WRITINGS FROM A GREEK PRISON

32 Steps, or Correspondence from the House of the Dead

Tasos Theofilou

Translated by Eleni Pappa
Preface by Ben Morea

ISBN: 978-1-942173-12-0
10 9 8 7 6 5 4 3 2 1

Dipli, dipli@espiv.net
dipli.espivblogs.net
commonnotions.org/dipli

Common Notions
314 7th St.
Brooklyn, NY 11215
www.commonnotions.org
info@commonnotions.org

Copyedited and proofed by Erika Biddle-Stavrakos. Special thanks to Siuloong Englander.
Cover photograph by Tasos Theofilou
Cover design by Josh MacPhee / Antumbra Design
Layout design and typesetting by Morgan Buck / Antumbra Design
antumbradesign.org

Printed in the USA / Printed in the USA by the employee-owners of Thomson-Shore
thomsonshore.com

IN MEMORY OF THE ANARCHIST CHRISTOS POLITIS (1979–2018)

About Dipli

Dipli [ΔΙΠΛΗ] is a Common Notions imprint on social cannibalism. Funds raised go to political prisoners.

> ΔΙΠΛΗ [DIPLI (/dip'li/): literally, double. The double telephone line is the way prisoners from different prisons communicate. Two to five prisoners from different prisons call the same telephone number at a pre-arranged time. The owner of that telephone number, living outside prison, connects them together.

Social cannibalism describes a situation in which people, individually or in small groups, oppress and exploit others in their immediate social environment and within the limits of their daily action. The most powerful ones attack the weakest with quotidian manifestations of domination, authority or influence. Social cannibalism is the lowest level of individualism in an increasingly fragmented society. It does not manifest immediately and completely but develops incrementally. Social cannibalism is the zero point of counter-revolution from below (through hierarchies, divisions, manipulations) just as war is the zero point of counter-revolution from above (through repression, recuperation, and mediation).

The term came into use with anarchists in Greece following the robbery and murder of Manolis Kantaris in Athens in November 2011. Golden Dawn, an ultranationalist, far-right political formation in Greece, exploited that incident to organize a pogrom against immigrants that led to the killing of Alim Abdul Manan on December 5, 2011. Social cannibalism has since come to signify a contradiction in which people who generally denounce violence accept it against those separated from themselves when executed by those connected to them. It also represents a pattern in which parts of the proletariat face off against one another by turning oppression of oneself into stigmatization of the other. Finally, social cannibalism embodies the political context of the European Union/European Central Bank/International Money Fund memoranda, in which the Greek Debt Crisis/Eurozone Crisis is homogenized according to nationality and then differently moralized, internalized into guilt of one's worth as a person through the relationship between self and other, and shared representations of action, emotions, and the body.

To publish on social cannibalism is to account for both the previous cycles of struggle in Greece and the global capitalist restructuring today.

dipli@espiv.net
dipli.espivblogs.net

Table of Contents

Preface

In a world built on exploitation there can be no guilt in resistance, likewise there are no innocent.

Ben Morea
New York, NY
July 2018

Editors' Note

Anarchist-communist Tasos Theofilou was arrested by the Greek Anti-Terrorist Unit on August 19, 2012. At the Court of First Instance (November 11, 2013–February 2, 2014), Theofilou was sentenced to twenty-five years of imprisonment for the charges of common complicity to homicide and the armed robbery of an Alpha Bank branch in Paros on August 10, 2012. He was acquitted of direct perpetration of homicide, joint constitution of and participation in the Conspiracy Cells of Fire (CCoF), and possession of explosives and "war material." At the Court of Appeal (November 21, 2016–July 7, 2017), Theofilou was acquitted of all charges. In 2018, Theofilou faced the danger of going back to prison due to an appeal lodged before the Supreme Civil and Penal Court of Greece [*Areios Pagos*] by one of its deputy prosecutors against the decision of his acquittal. The court rejected the appeal, and Theofilou was, definitively and irrevocably, acquitted of all charges. Theofilou spent five years in the prisons of Domokos and Korydallos. He was a member of the Network of Imprisoned Fighters and took part in a hunger strike (March 2, 2015–April 10, 2015) with a series of demands against the most recent punitive turn of the Greek penal system.[1] A wide solidarity movement supported Theofilou all these years.

The political case of Theofilou coincides with the implementation of the Economic Adjustment Programs (EAPs)—aka "the memoranda"—between the Greek state, the Euro-area member states, and the International Monetary Fund (IMF).[2] We can discern two distinct periods in how the EAPs are framed and moralized.

In the first period (2010–2015), which encompasses two EAPs, the Greek political personnel[3] framed the Greek crisis as one of competitiveness and sovereign debt, by linking it on the one hand to clientelism and rent-seeking and on the other hand to the Eurozone crisis and the global financial crisis. They moralized the crisis by coercing the population to internalize guilt

1. Abolition of Articles 187 ("Criminal Organizations") and 187A ("Terrorist Acts") of Chapter 6 ("Threats to Public Order") of the Penal Code; abolition of Articles 25 and 27 of Law 3772/2009 [which criminalized the use of any device that covers, hides or conceals a person's face]; abolition of "Type C" maximum security prisons; restricting the implementation of Article 200A ("DNA Analysis") of the Code of Judicial Procedure and its interpretation by the Public Prosecution Office of the Supreme Civil and Penal Court of Greece in Advice 15/2011 [in relation to forced extraction of DNA, use of mixed DNA samples, and presence of an expert witness on behalf of defendants in DNA analysis]; release of November 17 member and polytrauma patient, Savvas Xiros, in order to receive proper medical care.

2. First EAP (2010–2012); second EAP (2012–2015); third EAP (2015–2018).

3. Cabinet of George Papandreou (junior), Panhellenic Socialist Movement (October 7, 2009–November 11, 2011); coalition cabinet of Lucas Papademos, Panhellenic Socialist Movement – New Democracy – Popular Orthodox Rally (November 11, 2011 to May 17, 2012); cabinet of Antonis Samaras, New Democracy – Panhellenic Socialist Movement – Democratic Left (until June 25, 2013); Agreement for the New Greece (June 21, 2012–January 26, 2015).

and responsibility for it, while turning the parts of the population who did not fit or comply into a public enemy. Privatization and direct and indirect social wage cuts ran parallel to the racialized and gendered criminalization of HIV-positive persons, intensified policing of the Roma population and migrants, and the brutal repression of anti-memorandum opposition.

In the second period (2015–2018), the Greek political personnel[4] framed the Greek crisis as a humanitarian crisis, not by negating the framing of the first period but by linking it to the impact from the internal devaluation policy of the first two EAPs and the European migrant crisis. They moralized the Greek crisis by recuperating the anti-memorandum opposition, through the part of the population complacent enough to share responsibility for a national reconstruction plan and vote for and/or cooperate with the lesser of two evils. Structural adjustment, expansion of the population under workfare and/or NGOs/philanthropy, and over-taxation paralleled the promotion of a "social and solidarity economy."

We publish *Writings from a Greek Prison* by Theofilou to contribute to an understanding of social cannibalism from the perspective of prisonization—the extension of prisons and the lives they consume. We also want to draw attention to writings from the years of the memoranda that do not zero in on the social roles directly targeted by the EAPs, namely homeowners, self-employed or salaried workers, and welfare recipients. In this sense, the text by Theofilou is timely and rare. It provides an alternative angle on the years of the memoranda from the

4. First cabinet of Alexis Tsipras, SYRIZA – Independent Greeks – Ecologist Greens (January 27, 2015–August 28, 2015); second cabinet of Alexis Tsipras, SYRIZA – Independent Greeks (from September 23, 2015).

perspective of the "surplus population" in prison. The social relationships among inmates brings front and center a view of counterrevolution from below, while retaining in the background counterrevolution from above through the centrality of criminalization, penalization, and incarceration to contemporary capitalism.

What you hold in your hands is an English translation of the text "32 Steps, or Correspondence from the House of the Dead," in which Theofilou blends social commentary with three short stories, free verse, and a prison dictionary. Additionally, we include two letters written by Theofilou that contextualize his trial.

DIPLI editors
December 2018
Athens, Greece

Open Letter on the Commencement of the Trial at the Court of Appeal

November 2, 2016

On November 21st, after a nine-month postponement, my trial commences at the Court of Appeal. It's been two years since the completion of my trial at the Court of First Instance, when I was sentenced to twenty-five years imprisonment for the charges of common complicity to homicide and robbery in connection with the events on Paros Island on August 10, 2012. I was acquitted of participation in the Conspiracy of Cells of Fire as well as of direct perpetration of homicide by a majority opinion. It was a political (not judicial) compromise, resulting from a conflict between the manipulation of the case by the police in cooperation with the mainstream media during the first days after my arrest, the lack of any evidence, the solidarity expressed by the community, and the reaction of independent media.

From this emerged the temporary Solomonic solution of my partial acquittal of the charges, deferring the prospect of a conclusive decision until a trial at the Court of Appeal. There was an appeal initiated by myself, in which I upheld a full acquittal of all charges. There was also an appeal initiated by a gentleman called Δράκος [Dragon]—a public prosecutor whose surname obviously adds further symbolism to the witch-hunt orchestrated by the Anti-Terrorist Unit. Eventually, the division of opinion between the presiding judge, Mr. Hatziathanasiou—who voted for conviction on all charges—and the two other members of the court—who chose the more moderate option that eventually prevailed—made room for further manipulation. Mr. Δράκος, it would seem, felt that twenty-five years of imprisonment based on no evidence is not enough and went on to turn my trial at the Court of Appeal into a repetition of the initial trial. His appeal opened up the possibility of me not being fully acquitted or even facing a sentence harsher than life imprisonment.

I believe that the event of my arrest, its manipulation by the mainstream media, my detention and initial conviction highlighted certain issues that do not have to do with me personally. Rather, they bear a wider social and political importance. It is a manifestation of how a ruthless police state attempts to solidify the most extremist doctrines of judicial repression: from the medieval nature of my public castigation and the attempt to squeeze premodern criminal stereotypes into a fabricated profile; to the criminalization of friendship, comradeship or social relationships; as well as the use of supernatural or pseudoscientific evidence such as the notorious DNA on a hat, which forms the basis of this otherwise tragic story.

This latter aspect—the uncontrollable use of DNA—is one of the core issues that emerged and was to some extent restricted after the hunger strike of the members of the Network of Imprisoned Fighters. The question that arises is how the

Department of Forensic Examinations (DFE) can base their reports (and consequently how the court can possibly validate these reports through their decisions) on the Short Tandem Repeat (STR) method in order to identify offenders, when the developer of this method himself clearly states that it should only be used to disqualify suspects and not for identification purposes. How is it possible that this method is still used in Greece, when in the United States, the country that first introduced it in 1980, it's been deemed unreliable given the number of errors throughout the years? How is it possible that the laboratories of the DFE received an ISO certification only in 2014 while hundreds of people (myself included) had already been charged and convicted based on examinations that were conducted in uncertified laboratories?

In my case, there are specific circumstances that reveal an unrefined manipulation, since the one and only piece of evidence my conviction is based on is some genetic material detected on a hat—one that supposedly fell off a robber's head while he was fleeing. It happens to be a hundred-percent match to my genetic type. There are two important details though: (1) nothing can substantiate the fact that a hat fell off the perpetrator's head; (2) the photos of the crime scene taken by the police have captured every detail, however, no picture of this notorious hat seems to exist.

The hat appears in the photos of the findings taken at the Police Department of Attica (PDA). Based on the documents provided, it was sent to the PDA by the Police Department of Paros via post, on a different date and following a different route from the rest of the findings. Despite the manipulative questions formed by the presiding judge, Mr. Hatziathanasiou, and despite the illegal and admitted "preparation course" provided by the prosecution (a fact that Mr. Hatziathanasiou chose to gloss over with his sarcastic statement "no worries, this happens sometimes"), the prosecution witnesses' accounts contained so many inconsistencies that the very existence of this hat was never proven.

Secondly, the DFE report, which magically concludes that my DNA is a hundred-percent match, states that the inner side of the hat was tested with the use of cotton swabs but fails to specify the type of tissue tested. It does not mention if the tested sample was sweat, blood, sperm, skin cells, saliva or something else. The significance of this detail is expected to be known to even a first-year biology student, and even more so to a chief executive of the DFE. As a matter of fact, the report submitted by the DFE, which follows me in all the stages of this judicial procedure, from the interrogation, to the Court of Appeal, is brazenly inconclusive and in reality, compares my DNA sample (which was collected by means of violence at the Anti-Terrorist Unit premises) not to some other specified tissue but, literally, to thin air. Therefore, it comes as no surprise that this method revealed a hundred-percent match. And this is yet another reason why none of the DFE "scientists" dared to appear at court as witnesses to defend their bizarre theories. Because, had they done so, we would have come to the conclusion that even tarot cards are more reliable than the DNA methods used by the DFE.

My arrest is part of a crusade against the anarchist movement, launched and orchestrated by the law-and-order milieu: journalists, the Anti-Terrorist Unit, prosecution investigators, and wannabe Supreme Court judges. It is a crusade that dates back to 2009, when the dismantling of Conspiracy of the Cells of Fire was put forward as a pretext. A "vacancy" arose from the case of Nea Smyrni back in 2010.[1] A vacancy that the Anti-Terrorist Unit thought I "rightfully deserved," when in August 2012 a citizen was fatally injured in his attempt to prevent the escape of the robbers of Alpha Bank in Naousa of Paros Island. They based my "informed appointment" on an actual meeting I'd had back then [in 2010] with my friend and comrade Kostas Sakkas at an eatery in the neighborhood of Kallithea, as well as on an imaginary meeting with the then [in 2010] unknown to me but now comrade, friend and co-prisoner, Giorgos Karagiannides. It was a golden opportunity to slander the anarchist movement by profiling it as a mob of ruthless and bloodthirsty individuals.

It took the mobilization of all the mainstream media outlets broadcasting my arrest exclusively, striving to make the scenario appear plausible for a few days. For an entire week they presented me as a ruthless murderer. Photos of me went viral on the Internet while my commission to the courts on Loukareos and Evelpidon Streets, respectively, were broadcast live on all TV channels. In the name of law and order, judges, the media, and the police violated my rights and disgraced the famed presumption of innocence in every possible way. The media-cannibalism I was subjected to breached the aesthetic limits of the postmodern Dark Age we now find ourselves in.

Of course, it was not just the authority of the media that pursued my conviction by means of abusing even my written works and my private life, cramming criminal stereotypes into

1. Kostas Sakkas and Alexandros Mitrousias were arrested on December 4, 2010 outside a warehouse where weapons were found in the Nea Smyrni suburbs of Athens.

my fabricated profile (especially that of the paranoid murderer); jurisdiction followed suit as well. It's precisely the enforcement of media authority, after all, that made the lack of any evidence appear insignificant. Even the provocative statement at court: "Who knows, perhaps this man was not at the robbery," which came from the then-commissioner of the Anti-Terrorist Unit, Mr. Hardalias, was thought of as less of a scandal and more of a statement that shouldn't be noted in the minutes. It is a scandal because it was not just a statement that came out of his mouth spontaneously. It was a display of the power of a man and the service he represents in the space and time of a public trial. It is a scandal because he chose this arrogant way to manifest the absolute power that his service enjoys. He actually implied with cynicism: "I don't care if he was or wasn't at the robbery. I don't care about minor issues like evidence. I have my reasons to want him in prison. And he shall be in prison." This development came as no surprise given that the suppression of the anarchist movement had been assigned to the Anti-Terrorist Unit as its sole and exclusive responsibility.

The Anti-Terrorist Unit is a police service that enjoys provocatively preferential treatment by the media, to the degree that crime news informs case files and is considered valid evidence of guilt. Of course, we shouldn't have expected much more from the presiding judge, Mr. Hatziathanasiou, whose argument for my conviction on all charges went as far as to include the fact that I tend to use an electric razor—not a blade—during the freezing winter in Korydallos prison (meaning that, since one perpetrator appears to have no facial hair in the pictures taken by CCTV cameras and since he's disguised, then it must certainly be me!). He also felt the need to include that I haven't served in the Army and that I haven't read Genet's books. Needless to say he concurred with the draftsman of my criminal indictment, that my collection of fiction stories, Παρανουαρικό [*Paranoir*], as well as the crime reportage found in tabloids of the poorest quality, such as *Proto Thema*, should be considered valid documents substantiating my guilt. Likewise, we shouldn't be taken aback by the prosecutor, Mrs. Oikonomou's, attitude. She simply thought it was . . . appropriate or even in line with her responsibilities perhaps, to nap during most of the proceedings. It came as no surprise that she ended up reciting the document of my indictment when she was called to declaim her proposal.

These were, more or less, the conditions of my trial at the Court of First Instance. The political circumstances had placed the anti-terrorism witch-hunt at the top of the previous far-right government's agenda. The Minister of Justice and former public prosecutor, Mr. Athanasiou, announced his intentions to introduce high-security prisons for terrorists within the first one hundred days of his appointment. The Anti-Terrorist Unit arrested Kostas Sakkas every other day with silly pretenses, forcing him to become a fugitive.

Today the political circumstances are different. Even if the new government in power is in charge of implementing ruthless austerity policies, its audience is more progressive, which means the anti-terrorism/anti-crime/anti-immigration pledges are not put forward as top priorities. The government has symbolically (if not actually) invested in the repression of white-collar crime. This is the case despite the Ministry of

Justice's reluctance to openly confront the law-and-order lobby of the country. The Ministry of Justice uses deceitful tactics, voting for progressive laws and simultaneously using wording that allows judges to evade their imposition. They don't dare ensure that the rule of law applies in jurisdiction—it remains provocatively unregulated and open to extreme fundamentalist conceptualization, interpretation, and abuse of the monstrous Article 177 of the Criminal Procedure Law. This is related to the discretion thesis, which enables jurisdiction to be answerable not to what the law prescribes but to their personal ethics alone—ethics that are so sordid and vile that only Pontius Pilate would feel at ease with them.

These are the circumstances and these are the facts. I see my legal battle against all charges at the Court of Appeal as part of a wider battle against a ruthless police state, against judicial repression and its extremist doctrines. It is a bizarre existential battle in which adjudicators and prosecutors are parts of a single body—that of jurisdiction.

As I did at the Court of First Instance, I would like to highlight yet again that I don't pledge innocence and I will not plead with any judge to believe me. I am not innocent. In the class war, I've chosen a side. I stand with the underprivileged and the suppressed, the marginalized and the prosecuted, the transgressors and the accursed. I decided to take political action in the anarchist movement with the admittedly ambitious goal to strike down the social, political, and economic foundations of capitalism and its state. However, I denied, I deny, and will deny again all the accusations of the actions they've charged me with. I never was a member of the Conspiracy of the Cells of Fire, I didn't participate in this robbery and, above all, I never killed and wouldn't have ever been capable of killing an unarmed citizen for any reason or under any circumstances.

> For anarchy, for communism,
> Tasos Theofilou
> Korydallos prison

Statement on the Appeal Lodged Against the Acquittal Decision at the Court of Appeal

April 4, 2018

"In Athens today, 27th of March 2018, Tuesday 2 p.m., at the Public Prosecutor's office at the Supreme Court of Greece, the Deputy Prosecutor at the Supreme Court Ioannis Aggelis called me, the secretary of the Criminal Devision Georgios Sofroniades, and stated that he lodges an appeal before the Supreme Court of Greece, in accordance with the article 505, par. 2 of the Criminal Procedure Code, against the 2186/2017 (2938/16, 3303/16, 518/17, 565/17, 580/17) acquittal decision of the A' five-member Felony Appeal Court of Athens, whereof the accused Anastasios Theofilou was declared innocent."

That's the beginning of the number 21/2018 appeal statement, in which the prosecutor Mr. Ioannis Aggelis demands the annulment of the decision of the five-member Court of Appeal in Athens that acquitted me of all charges and remanded me to a new trial with different judges. Aggelis was recently promoted to the position of Deputy Prosecutor of the Supreme Court. Until then, he had been the supervising prosecutor of the "Anti-Terrorist Unit."

On the 11th of May, the appeal will be examined by a plenary session of the Supreme Court. If accepted, this means that I return to prison with the initial charges until the trial is repeated at the Court of Appeal with different judges, given that the majority of the A' five-member Court which acquitted me seems not to be to the liking of the Anti-Terrorist Unit.

As much as the Anti-Terrorist Unit and its surrounding circle of manipulated judges seem to have grown a somewhat obsessive dedication to my face, my case remains one that is not at all personal. It's political and pertains to the oppressive grip on the anarchist and the wider combative movement as well as our class as a whole. It's political since all the spearheads of this oppression were revealed socially and brought before social judgment, especially those related to the terror-law, the metaphysical use of DNA samples and the criminalization of social and political relationships. It's political because it gave prominence to the power and the social influence of the movement; because it proved that the Anti-Terrorist Unit and the judicial circles it manipulates are, if uncontrollable, not yet omnipotent. And that's what needs to be proved once again on the 11th of May.

PS: As once written by a comrade inside the Grevena prison: "Patience. Strength. Faith in the case. We are right. That's it!"

Tasos Theofilou
April 4, 2018

Translator's Note

My decision to translate this book stemmed from a feeling of emergency that bore in me as a reader. I find this is literature at its best, as the writer manages to depict society at its worst without resorting to an absolute rejection of what there is—it's not a nihilist's or pessimist's approach, as one might have expected. Disarming humor, sensitivity, and violent reality are united in one single body. The bleakest aspects of life in prison are described with a sobriety that one would expect to find in a detached observer's perspective. We see through thick walls. The spatial boundaries between "the in" and "the out" collapse. We're all confined. We're all subject to the very same restrictions regardless of where we might find ourselves—in prison or outside of it. The difference is in the intensity, the level of crudeness or sophistication. The rule of law, authority, and power are ruthless regulators of our behavior and the starting point of our battle against them is our awareness of this. We're all potential transgressors. This is why I felt that this book was worth sharing with the wider English-speaking audience.

Language-wise, I've felt that the whole translation endeavor was a precarious journey amidst the linguistic traps of the various "*English-es*" and English as an international language. Defining the audience was, in reality, impossible as I had no idea if, where or when the text would eventually be published. Should I make use of prison lingo equivalences that are found in prisons of a specific English-speaking country? Should I approach it from an international reader's perspective? But then again, there's no international version of English prison lingo, and the average reader is likely not familiar with their own country's prison slang.

The dictionary was the part I had to revisit over and over again. In the end, I resigned myself to the fact that this part of the book had to live up to the title it bears: it's a peculiar dictionary and its prime goal is to acquaint the reader—native English speaker or not—with the linguistic environment of Greek prisons without reducing its value as a piece of literature. The gap between the two types of discourse had to somehow get bridged. For this reason, I deemed it necessary to provide a simple phonetic script, both the literal and figurative meanings when needed as well as—more rarely—an English prison lingo alternative with an explanation. I hope the reader will find it enjoyable and informative despite the linguistic restrictions and the loose lexicographical style.

I would like to thank the writer, Tasos Theofilou, for discussing all the points that gave me trouble and contributing additional notes specific to the English-language version of his book. Special thanks to Christina Morrison and Christopher McCabe for their invaluable feedback. Many thanks to my good

Hanoian friends from Đội Cấn Street, Catherine Tomkins, Anemi Wick, and Linh Chi for being there.

In solidarity with Tasos Theofilou. In solidarity with all the political prisoners in Greece and elsewhere.

For a (prison-) free society.

Eleni Pappa
December 2016
Hanoi, Vietnam

32 Steps, or Correspondence from the House of the Dead

Prolegomena

Prison is a lot of things. Prison is shit. It is a black mark upon human civilization. It's a useless, relentless, psychological torment. Its interpretation, analysis, elaboration, and description are all multidimensional. These dimensions are political, social, economic, existential, psychological, sociological, cultural, and folkloristic. Not all of these dimensions can be described with equal precision.

Prison embodies a fundamental contradiction in that it integrates all those within the margins of society. It's positioned at the margins of populated areas, but simultaneously plays a core role in the functioning of capitalist societies. Prison is whatever it means for someone to have served there. It can't be described. "*He's served in prison*," means he's contaminated and pitiable, expiated and admirable. It's all of these together.

Prison's got a social role to play. It functions as an initiation with a full set of rituals to mark the stages of transposition. From being stripped of your clothes like fresh meat at first inspection—where you become reborn and fully conscious of your weakness before the power of correctionals[1]—to being set free again upon release. It comes with all the stages in between: trial, Court of Appeal, leaves, prison farm, the end. Prisoners acquire firm knowledge of hierarchy, obedience, ruthless rivalry, shafting, and fuckovery. All which we failed to internalize at school. A ritual in this transposition turns prisoners into anointed outlaws. We are initiated eventually, but not before being let in on all the secrets within this initiation—the experience of

[1]. Correctional officers.

deprivation, arbitrary prohibitions, imposed celibacy. We experience life between existence and nonexistence. It is life inspired by the routine and terminology of a monastery: the cell, the strict schedule, the deprivation, getting called *"brother."* The truth of capitalism is revealed in its full glory: the wretchedness of human beings; the misery of humanity in its most inglorious moments; the intertwining of black and legitimate markets; the hypocrisy of anti-crime rhetoric; Foucault's genius. The intermediation of authority in every trivial detail, the discipline, the absolute control.

Prisoners are forgotten people: incapacitated, miserable, nonexistent, and hidden. As if they were tailor-made to live here.

Prison is a different dimension of existence. Time is different. Neither slower nor faster, it's another dimension that can't be measured in hours. Measurements of time become the cell being locked and unlocked, the ration, the postman, the distribution of goods from the canteen, the cleaners' presence. This is how days and years alike are counted—with great patience, with the stages of our initiation. Court, Court of Appeal, leaves, prison farm, conditional release. The years go by and each of us has got something to wait for: Sunday's awful dessert, the canteen, the grocer, the visiting hours, the verdict of the Court of First Instance, a reduction of our sentence at the Court of Appeal, a better price for an aggregate sentence, the first leave, leaves in general, appealing for farm prison, a suspension, rarely a sentence termination. Years go by in agony—in sick agony.

Prison is forced cohabitation with people you haven't chosen. It's stale air. It's getting counted daily and locked up twice a day, like stock in a storage facility taken off the shelf for its habitual dusting and placed back again where it belongs. It's waiting for the postman. It's the always-empty phone card. It's never finding the time to say what you mean. It's just that some things can't be said on the phone. It's the visits. Long before you manage to acclimatize, time is up. By then, you've said nothing, of course. It's the melancholy when you get back to your cell, empty inside. And how could you ever quit smoking?

It's the loneliness, feeling that you're constantly carrying a gravestone on your lungs, yet you're sentenced to an absolute deprivation of personal time. There's always someone to pester you, someone to ask for a cigarette, some sugar, a spoonful of coffee. There's always someone who wants to share their pain— as if yours wasn't more than enough. Someone who wishes to keep you company—as if you'd ever asked for it. And it's the miserable sense of being eyeballed all the time, unable to take shelter behind a protective covering. If there's one thing prisoners and staff[2] alike know well, it's eyeballing. You're always naked in the cesspool.

Grey and white, iron and concrete, bars and aluminum. Suffocatingly limited space. Stifling yard. A pittance of sky with blades and wires. Pull-up bars, push-up bars, prison-made weights. Four sinks and three stoves. Plastic garden chairs. Plastic tables. Quaker oats, sesame paste, rice pudding, proteins, work outs, meal halvah, broomsticks, Atlacoll.[3] There are cameras and more cameras. "You'll get used to it," I was told on the first day. I still rue that happening.

The futility and sorrow felt when hugging your pillow at

2. Prison staff. See "υπάλληλος" in the dictionary, page 99.
3. Adhesive product, glue. See "Ατλακόλ," page 58.

night is unbearable. And there are the stories: tragic, tragicomic, real, plausible or delirious. Lots of stories. One prisoner—one story, one prisoner—many stories. Shaggy-dog stories.

Each block is a whole little universe and a small neighborhood. The neighbors are somewhat eccentric. Just like the little gentleman across from my cell. He blasted two with a shotgun over landownership disputes. "This story has dragged on since my grandma's years," he explains. Or the sweet-tempered, sixty-year-old vegetarian fellow who does yoga every morning. He's a hitman—best of his generation. He's patient, methodical, and precise. "Bushman" is what he's called in his absence. Nearby stands the dope dealer, he's a good fellow, extremely courteous. Further down you'll find a short hairy guy. He's got a hairy back and a face that inspired Lombroso.[4] Some indefinable, worn off, badly made tattoos on his hands and decorative scars on top of some them—a product of his attempts to get rid of the tattoos. He's a lifer too. He killed his lover because he'd been cheating on him. Stabbed him more than twenty times. "The key is to avoid the first stab altogether," he explains, "then your mind just goes blurry and you don't understand." He's a punch in the gut to any gay stereotype. And there's the guy with the high-pitched voice, round belly, and red cheeks. He's so placid. He was sentenced three times to life imprisonment, one for each murder. Committed on the spur of the moment. A moment of impulsiveness equals a lifetime in prison. "Strange folks, those hunters," he explains. "I used to be one of them so I know first-hand. I told them not to trespass on my field. They left their

4. Cesare Lombroso (1835–1909), Italian criminologist and physician, founder of the Italian school of Positivist Criminology.

scent and my herd wouldn't graze. I told them time and again. Strange folks those hunters are. They think they've got a gun and rule the world. Well, that's not how the story goes. They're not the only ones bearing guns," he comments blissfully while gazing at a small patch of sky.

Stories of uprisings

"Back then, you'd have to file an application to make a phone call; you had to visit the sergeant's office and call in his presence. That's where the visiting hours were arranged. Having visitors was way more difficult and restricted. The service[5] controlled our mail. There were no TVs, just a few small ones that ran on batteries for an hour only. Each cell was provided with two batteries. One would be handed over to one of the staff for charging when the other was in use.

Leaves, suspensions, barely edible food, radio, TV, telephones. We gained all these as well as being respected by the service. Back then they were extremely provocative. You wouldn't even dare look at them in the eyes. And there were the disciplinary prisons: Corfu, Larissa, Diavata.[6] Solitary confinement. Impalements with batons. Being tied to the cross.

The food was cooked in cauldrons and only served on trays on Sundays. When the uprising kicked off, one team took over the pharmacy and another, the kitchen. We were unable to take the gatehouse—we got stopped. We took some hostages, too. Among them was a sub-sergeant; we put him in Block D, cell number 120. Two prisoners supervised him. The majority of the rest had swallowed pills from the pharmacy and caused trouble. They wanted to slaughter him, but in my view, that wasn't the point. The point was to make ourselves heard. At the sight of knives, the sub-sergeant shat his pants and a prisoner gave him clean underpants to wear. We had to get

5. Prison service. See "υπηρεσία," page 99.

6. These prisons are named after the provinces they're located in.

him to the front gate every three hours so that they could see he was OK.

We took petrol from the kitchen to make Molotov cocktails and poured some in the corridors to stop the riot police from getting in. We also released the minors from the juvenile correction institute, which was housed in what's now Block E. That's how the minors joined the uprising. They started fighting both with one another and the service.

We took turns in shifts to keep watch on the terrace. Police helicopters were hovering above our heads throwing tear gas. "There will be blood, you won't take back the prison," we said.

We overtook the kitchen and organized our meals on our own despite the shortages. We used the loudspeakers to talk to the women's prison.

Some prisoners were unable to endure the uprising. It was a hardship. We'd run out of mattresses as we'd burnt them all, there wasn't much food, and some joined the side of service to seek protection. Those we called grasses,[7] but in my view that wasn't the point.

All prisons were destroyed. Correctional law was changed and telephones were installed. As the time went by and more uprisings took place, the correctionals' attitude changed too. The food improved but later worsened again. The prison itself worsened. We had both grasses and *servicials*[8] but we knew who was who in the past. Things were clearer back then, more of a family affair."

7. See "Ρουφιάνος (/rufi'anos/)": grass, page 88.
8. A prisoner who's on good terms with the prison service, especially the sergeant. See "Υπηρεσιακός (/ipiresia'kos/)": "servicial," page 99.

Stories of Albania

We were children in Koritsa and it was Easter. It was a bunch of us. We wanted to roast a goat just like the adults did. We went down to the goat shed to steal one but the goatherd noticed and started chasing us. He nearly got me but a friend threw a stone in his direction to save me. He fell down. We thought he was just playing dead. I grabbed a stone and killed the goat. I loaded it on my shoulders and off we went. Going down the mountain, we were noticed and recognized. I left and spent half a year in Greece, waiting for things to die down. I came back for a gas station robbery we'd organized but by that time it'd been closed down. I saw a car just like my father's. My father's car had no windscreen or battery and that year it was a heavy winter. I pulled out my knife and tore the rubber from the windscreen. While busy tearing, I heard a voice. The owner of the car was inside, napping. I took a closer look and realized he was a schoolmate of mine from primary. "Fucking cunt," I said, "I'll just take the windscreen and the battery. I won't hurt you." Later, the cunt screwed me because he'd recognized me. They were after me.

I didn't spend much time in prison. I was a minor, they had no evidence for the murder, and an uncle of mine was a member of Berisha's party.[9] There, the chambers hosted fifteen inmates and were underground. There was no toilet. We pissed in a cauldron that we emptied every night and shat in plastic bags behind a towel held by two others like a screen. The shit bags were hurled out of the bars. We passed our time playing

9. Sali Berisha (born 1944), president of Albania from 1992 to 1997 and Prime Minister from 2005 to 2013. Leader of the Democratic Party twice, 1991–1992 and 1997–2013.

Biriba.[10] Radio was not allowed. One day they found my secret radio, they took it away and sent me to the disciplinary cell for two days. I was only fifteen years old. I wanted to listen to music. Not even mail was allowed and we sent out our letters wrapped in the silver paper of the cigarette packet. Showers were a hardship too. Albanian winter. Each of us would place a bottle of water between his legs and with a little help from the blanket and a little help from our farts, by the next morning the water would have warmed up. Not hot. Every day one of us would have a shower."

10. A card game.

Stories of crimes that never made the headlines

I'm in cell number forty-eight. The cleaners get locked back in, I dig out my phone from its hole and talk by the window. My cellmate says "inspection." I bury it back in. I take out my little mirror and see there's an inspection in cell 80. It strikes me as odd to see the staff wearing jackets in spring. I dig out my mobile again and as I'm talking, I notice someone from Block A shouting, "fire!" I take out my mirror and see smoke coming out of cell 80. We knock down the door. Within the next five minutes I see flames coming out and all the way up to the ceiling. The whole prison is shouting. The staff comes without his key, then returns with it but can't open the door. All this happened within a quarter of an hour. They opened the adjacent cells to stop them from getting burnt down too.

They had no water, the fire extinguishers were empty, water was only to be found in the kitchen. So, we tried to put out the fire using pots. Within fifteen minutes everything had melted down.

The door opened and we saw three prisoners hugged together, clutching onto the window in an attempt to save themselves. Coal. The fourth one we saw was coal black below his neck, his head unscathed, breathing heavily. He died in the hospital. We went to collect the burnt bodies but they had been stuck to the bars. The block was fucked up.

We tried to revolt. We locked the entrance to the block and cut the window bars so we could climb up to the rooftop. The sergeant tried to buy us off with pills. We reckoned the service had deliberately caused this to happen—that the prisoners knew something and wanted to negotiate. That's not the way a cell gets burnt down. Everything had burnt down within a quarter of an hour.

In the end, we broke. They brought in the Special Suppressive Counter-Terrorism Unit and the riot police, got us out naked, and beat us up one by one. They just covered it up. No one said a word.

———

The sense of confinement is not of minimal importance. It's the deprivation of any potential to escape or concede. As if all the other great many deprivations aren't enough. You're doomed to cope with everything and learn the language of both the prisoners and the service. You learn to speak their language. The language of thugs, of underlying meanings, of power, innuendos, deals, authority, hierarchy, fuckovery. And you need to become fluent yet never let it become your mother tongue. They ran an inspection in an Albanian's cell and found a knife, an edged blade, almost like a sword.

"What's this?" they asked.
"What is it?" he replied. "Can't you see? It's a calculator."
"What sort of calculator is this," the country bumpkins wondered.
"One that helps me to keep track of my accounts. It's applied math."

These people in here are humans. They're normal humans, with flesh, bones, and souls. They experience confinement in each of the cells of their body. Moment by moment, day by day, year by year. And there are those who led them in here. Humans tied them up, humans sentenced them, and humans guard them. And they are all equally tainted. Saints and sinners are all in the same boat. Foucault grins.

The 32 steps at the yard. Up and down, up and down like a robot. How much pain can be squeezed into 32 steps, how much injustice, how much poverty, how many personal dramas, how many family tragedies, how much suppression, how much life in condensed form?

"We're bereft of affection," that's what I was told by a young Algerian convicted for robberies back in 2003. "Back then, I was eleven years old," he complained to me as if there was anything I could do about it. "I hardly even knew there was a country called Greece." This, of course, didn't bother the judges who gave him an ample fifteen to relieve the police of paperwork. "*God gemi years to live and yo ja stretcha handa grab five?*" mused a soft-eyed Bulgarian. Eighteen years in prison just because. "With the labor days, Courts of Appeal, suspensions, you won't stay in for more than five years," explained the experts trying to console him. "*God gemi years to live and yo ja grab five wida a movement?*" he repeated. That's all the substance of criminal justice. Condensed truth. All's condensed. Condensed truth, condensed wisdom, condensed experience, condensed space, condensed depression, condensed scenery; even ejaculation is condensed.

We have a gravedigger on the block. His demeanor embodies the archetype: emaciated, tall and toothless, with a big hooked nose. He used to work for a municipality. "It was a good job," he said. "A salary of one thousand and four hundred euros, plus almost two hundred in lucky tips when the dead were young. I had such a good time! After the funeral, I'd take them to a café for cognac, I'd collect my commission from the café, and they treated me to free booze. Then, at the family's house they treated me to cod. I had a good time. Later at night, I'd open the coffin—to avoid being noticed—and collect all their gold. Watches, bracelets, teeth; I smuggled them all down in Omonia Square.[11] Heavy and tough work this was, opening the coffin of young people. You need to have soul." "You need to have no soul," I replied.

Announcements never stop. "Cleaners! Put the bins out." "Cleaners! Bring the bins back in." "Commissary worker! Go to the watch." "Gummy! Go to the watch." "Whatsyourname! Go to the watch." "Busboys! Collect the trays." "Stewards! Serve the trays." When will the prison open? Let us out! Let us sling our hooks! Ruled with a rod of iron—a reminder of what this culture has produced. "Those who want a haircut, go to the recreation hall." "Hairdresser! Take a break." Commands drone on until prisoners comply. Until they become incapable of acting on their own will.

The guy looks like a wrestler. His shaved head is crowned with scars and marks of stitches. He's over forty and has served more than twenty years since he was eighteen, with little reprieve. "I'm my mom's pride. Prison to home, home to prison," he brags. We sit around the little table and he reels off his

11. Omonia Square is one of the most central squares in Athens, formerly known as "Palace Square."

stories. He killed one, he stabbed the other. He's wearing slippers and his little toes are hooked over his fourth toe on each foot. "Why are your toes like this? Your high heels got them crooked?" I ask. He laughs. "It's my wrestling shoes," he replies. Fortunately, he has a sense of humor and doesn't treat me to a stab as a souvenir.

There's a very particular feeling prison generates, one that can't be found outside. A tide caused by deprivation of freedom, hopelessness, walls, wires, nonstop coercion, nonstop control, imposed cohabitation, monotony, continuous assertion of space, eternal anticipation of something, a relentless walk on a fine line, the prison's schedule, nostalgia, hope. The eternal torment of confinement. Prison means accumulated anticipation, accumulated devastation, accumulated injustice. Tough luck, sadism, suppression, prohibition, coercion, all are accumulated. Anxiety, distress, body index, sighs, tension, commands, desperation, loneliness, abandonment, punches on the punching bag, psych drugs, repetition on the pull-up bars, TV, folk-pop music, up and down on the pull-up bar, up and down on the push-up bar, patience, meaningless and insipid conversations in broken Greek. All is accumulated.

Accumulated stories. Stories here, stories there. Stories everywhere. "The cops get me in the panda car and drive me to the station. I'd swallowed a Vulbegal[12] and kleptomania took over me. I see the cop's mobile phone and snaffle it. I put it in my sock. The phone rings. He's looking for it. '*Where's the phone, where's the phone, you got it, cunt! No, dudes, you got it.*'

12. A benzodiazepine sedative and hypnotic drug, elsewhere known as Flunitrazepam or Rohypnol, aka benzos, roofies, the "date-rape drug." Criminal behavior is listed among other "paradoxical effects"!

They search me and find it. They beat the fucking shit out of me. They say, '*Inside your sock, fucking cunt!*' while beating the shit out of me. He didn't take the call. '*In the sock, fucking cunt.*' Shit more beat up. At the station he cleaned it with a wet napkin before taking the call. That was a fucking beat up, fucking hell."

The reality in prison makes my eyes callous. People end up here due to a ruthless sway, due to a voracious power which respects only power. In here, you see all the putridity of capitalism being reproduced on the crudest and most inhuman terms. On the other hand, you see prisoners in such restricted space pretending to live, and eventually, some manage to do so. Eventually they live. From inside deathly walls life emerges in the form of a weed, watered with pain, tension, injustice, and anticipation. Life sprouts and grows roots inside concrete. You see people struggling to stay alive and some do. You see a whole new civilization develop, a dehumanized, succinct reflection of society. There's crudeness without pretext. Nevertheless, it's a whole new culture on the margins of society and under the pointed heel of authority.

The overtly class-based operation of criminal justice becomes so apparent in here. A poor man's lot is tough. There's a gypsy. He doesn't know when he was born. He doesn't know how to make a phone call, he can't read the symbols of the numbers so he asks others to press the buttons for him. In for seven years already, serving seventeen total for a robbery. He entered a bakery unarmed, he took twenty euros from the cashier, a transistor radio found nearby, and then asked for a loaf of bread. He got caught, trialed, forgotten. He's served them seven years and counting.

Prisoners say: "I've served *them*" however many years. It means: I did it for the establishment because *they* forced me to do it. That's underlying class-consciousness; or class-unconsciousness, rather.

While making his coffee, someone turns to me and says: "It's the prisoners that make you hate prison, it's not the bars and the walls. Prison is tough but bearable. It's the people inside that make it unbearable." It's true that the ranks of the subproletariat are a shitty lot. But then again, workers built this place, the middle classes designed it, and I wouldn't be feeling any better in a cage full of the nouveau riche.

The other one never works out. He can't because his legs are crippled. They shot him repeatedly upon his arrest. Now, it's his third year inside. He's started walking. He got an eighteen-year sentence. "First, they cripple you, then they bury you alive," he says, laughing. Eighteen years for attempted murder because, when arrested, the bullet was inside the gun chamber. He didn't shoot, but he had the bullet in the gun chamber. Three coppers shot him, three coppers arrested him, and subsequently he was charged with multiple attempted murders. Unfortunate story. He was sleeping with his Tokarev under his pillow because of past troubles. Three men in civvies got into his house; he grabbed his pistol and ran. It turned out the fellows were from the Drug Enforcement Coordination Unit. They found nothing, not even a joint, but they crippled him and treated him to a sweet eighteen years.

And there's the other one who has no teeth. Prisons are places where the average number of teeth per mouth is even smaller than in nursing homes. That's due to substance abuse. This fellow is around thirty-five and has no front teeth whatsoever. He's in for possession of a number of kilos of weed. "Did you use to do dope?" I ask. "No," he replies, "never, only weed." "And how come you have no teeth left?" I ask, employing all that's left of my tact. "Some fell because of the sugar but most of them I lost during the interrogation." He dumbfounds me.

Taking walks at night. That's what I've missed. The scents of the city, the mountains, the sea, the night. The night's sounds. Gazing at the stars instead of blinding headlights. Sitting somewhere after eight. To be neither counted nor locked. To drink a beer and gaze at the stars.

Prison is not really a big deal. They simply take you and plant you inside concrete and iron and you have to try to remain blossomed, seeing some people around you can't make it. You see them wither and you get scared. And you desperately try to remain in your friends' lives but the phone-card credit is never enough. You have to pluck up your courage at all times, you share courage with your people outside, you can't be defeated; even the least important verbal fallacy bears a huge weight. You're dependent and liable.

Then, years and years will have passed—inevitably they will—and you'll have to adapt to the outside. You'll have to be something more than a voice at the other end of the line between eight and twelve or three and eight, you'll have to be a person that actually exists. You'll have to invade their lives just because. Because that's what you left behind, without asking if they want you back. One says with his eyes almost wet: "Had a visit from my daughter. Hadn't seen her for five years. I felt ashamed. She's a proper woman now. I felt ashamed." The torment of confinement lasts forever, not only for as long as you're sentenced. And life goes on amidst a grey background. Neither slower, nor faster. Not the same.

———————

They inform me that I'm about to be transferred. I leave Korydallos.[13] Back to my grey grave. Korydallos is a bearable prison. Despite its third-world conditions in terms of hygiene, nutrition and accommodation, it still has some human elements. It was built in an era when physical violence was the means of controlling and managing the prisoners. The need for sadistic architecture found in modern prisons had not yet emerged. Korydallos is a big prison. Its inmates are under trial—meaning fresh—so they haven't completely lost contact with society. It's the mother of all prisons, without extreme prohibitions, without many taboos. All the new trends start from here and what happens here is of greater importance.

It's got a big yard, soil on the ground, trees and flowers, berms and kiosks and benches. And the walls are made of stone, not concrete, and the floor is mosaic, not glossy grey. It's interesting, in the way museums are, as so many household names have served here, both political and criminal outlaws.

There are lots of cockroaches in Korydallos, a vast number of them. They never go away. They make an appearance literally everywhere: on the pillows, in the soup, in shoes, inside the screen of the pay phone, between the digits of the credit and the

13. Korydallos prison is the main prison complex in Greece. It's located in Piraeus.

duration of call indicator. It's kind of like modern art. Prisoners chase them. Cockroaches have been ruthlessly tailed, even if they're the least harmful creatures in this place, even if they're entitled to own this space. We always claim this place shamelessly and always take advantage of the weaker.

I leave the metropolis behind me. The police van for special transfers is waiting for me at the gate. My escorts, after conducting the necessary body cavity inspection, show me to my place. It's a small metal cage the size of a phone booth with a small metal stool for me to sit on. There are small pillows on the front and back to ensure that I don't arrive as damaged goods. Despite the futuristic apparel of my escorts, I won't be teleported but simply transferred with all the care non-fragile merchandise deserves. My cage boasts small holes on its metal sheet, which serves as a sliding door. I can see outside. I'm trying to absorb as many snapshots as possible. Blocks of flats, stores, cars, people. Life goes on without me, for as long as we're in Athens. I can see the horizon for a while on the Athens-Lamia Highway. I don't really know when the next time will be. The van is speeding like crazy and I bump around all over the place. If I had a sticker with *fragile* on me, they wouldn't be driving so recklessly.

We arrive within two hours. Back to Domokos.[14] I get unloaded. They sign invoices, delivery notes, who-knows-what documents and leave me waiting. Then, after they've completed the procedural inspection, I ask them to get me to a different block. "Why the hell was I put in the Russian one? I can't speak the language!" I protest. "Fair enough, that was a great prank. You got me. But that's enough." They agree. They take me to the Greek

14. A prison named after the small provincial town of Domokos, located in central Greece.

block. I get in. It's the very same architecture, a two-story grey mass with ten heavy iron gates on each floor. A double-decked space with twenty lockers for human storage and three dwellers in each locker. That's it, enjoy! It's a solid structure to guarantee absolute control, with consideration for nothing else whatsoever. Nothing like emotions, scenery, images, smells, and the like. Criminals deserve none of these. Not even a blind spot, a totally controlled space, there are cameras everywhere. Transparency. A grave for the living. Here people are sentenced to dwell for countless years. The same architecture and design as in my previous block. A different world, though. Every block is a different universe. The difference lies in the synthesis of individuals, the so-called "material." This gives each block a different dimension. There are many former minors in this block who pass down customs and traditions. Prisons for minors are harsh. The block is divided into thugs[15] and fraggles.[16] In reality, prison is not home to the most dangerous ones but the least competent at avoiding it. However, they're very good at surviving in this environment and usually incapable of surviving anywhere else.

I have yet to grasp the social role of subproletarians. I might as well undermine their ethics and code of conduct owing to my Marxist snobbishness or my middle-class naivety. Or, it could actually be the reverse. Prison and the stories about its people are sometimes exotic and lyrical. More often than not, however, they're simply bleak. It just goes to show that all the cruelty imposed from above is reproduced inside among the lowest ranks of society.

15. See "σπαθόλουρο," page 90.
16. See "αδυναμία," page 51.

Boubi's case is exemplary. Boubi is not his real name. It's a name chosen to reinforce his role. You'll see him with red fingermarks on his neck and cheeks. Sometimes the bashes he gets resonate all over the block and, therefore, turn into big shindigs. Boubi just goes teary-eyed but never protests. He ducks slavishly and walks away. No matter where he is, bashes and orders come and go: "I've got some dirty underwear, by tomorrow I want them washed and hung" or "I've left pots and dishes in the sink for you to wash" or "you didn't wash them properly, you fucking cunt, they're still oily." More bashes come and go. Boubi ducks again and washes even more zealously.

"Why didn't you come over to my cell to check if I needed anything?"
"Because I'd been feeling unwell."
"What was it, your period?"

And here comes a bash as a treat. Those who don't do bashes restrict themselves to ousting him whenever they see him.

The official excuse is that he's a grass. *"During the interrogation, he got beaten coz he wouldn't stop speaking . . ."* This is the case for half of the block's dwellers but he was so naïve that he admitted it. The truth is he suffers it all because he's weak and, to some extent, tolerant.

He hesitates to react, he says, for fear of getting beaten. He fears things could get even worse but he doesn't know there can't be anything worse than this. He's not one of the service's grasses. Service somehow manages to keep their grasses well protected. Unless their authority is questioned or the normal operation of the prison is impeded, they don't bother. They just let it happen. The good kings who redress injustice exist only in fairytales. In here, we find ourselves in Plato's dystopia, in his ruthless Republic, and we're in its most tainted caste. Utterly dehumanized by the subject of authority, we're the iron ones that live within concrete and iron. The silver caste—that of the guards—just ensures the imposition of order. As for the golden caste—not philosophers but pen pushers, public prosecutors, executives—they simply rule from the security of their offices.

"How do you like our corner shop?" he asks me. He has the face and flair of someone who's served in minors. A contradiction of childishness and cruelty is inscribed on his face. The abrupt eradication of any childishness has left its imprint forever. His face is of indefinite age. I'd believe him should he claim anywhere between twenty and forty. I'd never ask though. Perhaps he mostly looked for answers—not questions—while keeping his reps on a prison-made workout bench. The weather was gloomy and chilly. Rain and melancholy drizzled down. It reminded me of rainy days at school when breaks were wasted in classrooms. Smells, sounds, feelings, all resembled a rainy morning at school—without the threatening anticipation of a ringing bell, of course.

"How am I supposed to like it?" I respond in puzzlement. (Honestly, how could I ever like it? What else could I ever think—it's shit.)
"We're peaceful in here," he says.
"Yeah, I know," I reply.

"You gonna get your ass fucked, fucking cunt!" he shouts, chasing Andreas, hurling pots and pans in his direction. Everyone knows it's Andreas' fault and everyone knows he's not really in danger. He runs in his slippers, with his toes sticking out. That's as close to his shoe size as he could get. Those who have no money or visitors are doomed to make do with what's rarely superfluous to the rest of the prisoners. He keeps running, splashing through the water on the floor in his slippers and as soon as he's at a safe distance, he stops and declares like a proper toff, hoping to placate his pursuer: "You're a proper gentleman." A second round of chasing kicks off only to pause for a clarification: "with a capital G."

Andreas has been in for about four years now on numerous small sentences, which he's now, in his senility, accumulated as a petty thief. He stands near the yard gate wearing a white jacket, a blue shirt, orange shorts, and a pair of comfortably worn-down slippers. Whenever a prisoner steps out, Andreas welcomes him with a battler's smile: "Good morning sir, you're the best in the west," only to get the usual response: "Go to hell fucking cunt." His bald head, thin gray hair, and sweet old face are enough to repeatedly save him from the worst since they evoke mercy or even affinity.

"Give me an orange," he asks, starting to massage you on the spot. Massage is a valued service in prison. He exercises pressure on your palm, between the thumb and the pointer, and asks if it's painful. As soon as you say yes, his expression becomes portentously serious, like a doctor's, and he offers his medical opinion: "You haven't had sex recently, that's it!" He keeps on with the massage and when you're just about to relax, he stops and says:

"That's all you get for free, give me an orange." You give him the orange and he goes off to trade it for a cigarette, which he trades for a cup of clothes detergent, which in turn is traded for twenty cents on the phone card. After he's triggered this exchange (one that's beneficial to all) he uses his twenty cents to call his mom and ask for pocket money. "Imagine having a son like him," someone remarks, "a son who's sixty years old and calls you from prison to ask for pocket money."

I observe Andreas from the window of my cell during the Sunday lunch booze session. Five or six criminals are hidden in a cell. It feels like the Prohibition era. He's found a ladybug again, which he protectively places in the safety of a small grassy corner. Satisfied, wearing a smile of semi-madness, he continues his monotonous stroll through the yard. "What is he in prison for?" I ask myself for a moment only. "What are any of us in prison for?" I correct myself while observing our fellowship as we risk suffering a disciplinary punishment for poisoning ourselves on prison-made booze.[17] We've frozen it in an attempt to feel less of what we're pouring in our guts, defying the hangover. Prison is an endless mass hangover. Five or six of us drink and eat together at a Sunday get-together. We haven't put on our smart clothes. The rules of social decency are paralyzed by the power of routine. We're dressed in slippers and short pants and have nasty tattoos on our bodies.

Some sausage, tomatoes, onions, and feta cheese we'd kept from last night's ration, that's all our Sunday food. Ali doesn't eat sausage because it's made of pork. "Have mine, it's beef," someone offers, only to get us all laughing out loud and trigger

17. See «Τσίπουρο (/'tsipuro/)»: brew, page 97.

the usual teasing reserved for Muslim prisoners who comply with abstinence from pork but don't care about alcohol prohibitions. We're in prison, where Allah turns a blind eye. The Nigerian of the fellowship has undertaken the distillation of this alcoholic mix made of oranges and peaches. Thus, the common title "doctor"—attributed to whoever undertakes this post—has now turned into "Yacoub," for self-evident skin-color reasons.[18]

Yacoub participates in the fellowship only physically. He speaks only the basic Greek words which are just enough for him to cover the very basic prison needs. This is his vocabulary: leave, suspension, prison farm, trial, public prosecutor, sergeant, clerk, postman, postal order, card, coffee, tobacco, cigarette, booze, broom, dry, food, labor days, pot, cunt, prison in, prison out, water, yard, and toilet. He doesn't always get the pronunciation right. Nevertheless, some do speak to him while he pretends to be listening attentively, nodding with interest in what they might be saying. He's vigilant and when his interlocutor laughs, he laughs back, pretending to understand. He's in for drug dealing. He got caught in a park, carrying a massive seven grams of hash, and was sentenced to twelve years imprisonment. Misfortune dogs the downtrodden, so to speak. It's not only Greek criminal justice that has been ruthless towards him. His torment continues inside the prison as he's forever falling prey to the slickest of tormenters. For instance, he's been told that "fucked up" means fucked from above and that's a derogatory expression while, on the other hand, "fucked down" is an

18. Inspired by Sir Magdi Habib Yacoub, a famous British-Egyptian cardiothoracic surgeon who operated on A. Papandreou—Greek Prime Minister from 1981 to 1989 and 1993 to 1996. Greek society, back then, viewed Black people as exotic. Anyone with even a slightly darker-tone complexion was thought of as Black!

honorary one. So, whenever a troublemaker teasingly tells him "you're fucked up," he takes offense and responds passionately: "Me no fucked up, me fucked down." The same applies in cases when he's called a cunt. He denies it emphatically: "Me no cunt, me little tart." What's definitely sad is that no one, myself included, has ever gotten around to sorting things out and explaining all these to him.

Boozing continues, tuned to the sound of Zafeiris Melas' "*Don't tell me you love me coz am gonna believe it.*" It's a masterpiece of mainstream pop-folk music, or perhaps it's just the effect of prison on my taste in music.[19] Yacoub is dancing the *Zeibekiko*.[20] The rest are cheering and clapping their hands. We're obviously out of control. "There's no sausage left," one prisoner complains only to get his complaint addressed: "You can have mine. It's been in prison for so long, it looks like a proper sausage." Laughter.

It's the least homogeneous gathering. Prison is a big melting pot: outlaws, body building, cocaine, dope, show biz, police, crimes of passion, anarchists, robbers, thieves, smugglers, smuggled work force, smuggled cigarettes, smuggled petrol, drugs, businessmen, politicians, poor devils, pickpockets, and junkies. All mixed in the penal bin.

The only common point of reference in this heterogeneous bunch is our confinement and, consequently, the common needs it generates. A German lifer and drug smuggler, a Pakistani hash dealer, a Nigerian hash smoker, an anarchist, and finally, a former traffic warden convicted for car theft.

19. Melas is a popular singer, highly appreciated in the pop-folk subculture.
20. A pop-folk dance.

"This is," he says, "what policing is. The drug squad sells drugs, the anti-extortion department extorts people, and so on and so forth. I was a traffic warden, what else could I do?" he complains through laughter. "I stole cars." And there stands Giorgos. His father is a sailor from Samos and his mother is from Singapore.[21] There, in the wilds of Asia, he served his first sentence. He was a minor back then, and one of the few who's got memories of the ball and chain when he was brought to work in the fields. Now he's in his fifties but his muscles bulge under his exotic skin. I observe his biceps and gauge that they're somewhat bigger than my calves. Since the nineties he's been in and out (mostly in, less out) of Greek prisons but he only complains about his last sentence. The lawyer was straightforward: "*All the evidence is against you.*" "Which evidence exactly?" he wondered. "I was caught a kilometer away from a robbery. I carried no gun, nothing. Which evidence? I was just walking." "*You've got a criminal record and your face looks criminal,*" his lawyer reassured him. *Justice is ok.*

I'm drunk and my eyes are cast outside the window again. Andreas is not out there at the moment and the spiral bladed wires are twinkling spitefully under the midday sun. I'm wondering, "For how much longer?" and feeling gloomy. He looks at me and nods in agreement: "Fuck it, too much prison!"

They didn't let us out on time. It's nine and the counting hasn't started yet. I've been pacing up and down in the cell for an hour. They must be running an inspection somewhere. Five minutes later, a guard unlocks and counts in haste. Shortly afterwards, the head cleaner appears and comes in. His is

21. Samos is a Greek island located northeast in the Aegean Sea.

a fearsome figure. When you see him, oh, you back off, you don't want to mess with him. He's good, almost kindhearted, but his appearance . . . . He's bald, wrestler-like, dark-skinned, nasty prison-made tattoos, swollen muscles, you just back off. You don't mess with him. Now he's wearing a tight "Punisher"-stamped t-shirt and army boots instead of shoes. Cleaners behind him are carrying his mighty load of paraphernalia: buckets, brooms, mops, squeegees, and floor detergents. They don't seem particularly sullen, depressed or fearful.

"Where have you been?"
"Cleaning the block next door."
"How come? No cleaners there?"

They'd been called in with the first cockcrow of the day. Before the prison opened. They cleaned up the blood with the squeegees and sterilized the room. The aftermath: one dead, two in the hole (meaning the disciplinary guard room, also known as solitary confinement). They'd been boozing the previous night. They argued, fought, pulled out knives, and that's it. A drunken argument, squared to the power of pressure resulting from confinement. A nasty hangover.

Waking up after a drunken night to realize you didn't simply quarrel more than you should have, you didn't simply confide in someone you shouldn't have, you didn't simply dance on the tables. It's waking up to feel alcohol instead of blood running through your veins; alcohol and curse. Waking up to realize that after having spent eighteen years in prison looking forward to your release, you've now treated yourself to another twenty. Waking up to realize that two lives were wasted on the spur of the moment.

No one called him a murderer or killer. This highly charged discourse doesn't belong here. There are neither killers nor murderers to be found in here. There are prisoners serving their sentence for homicide. He was called by his name, Kostas, and everyone agreed he'd acted in a shitty way. Some had met him on other blocks in other prisons. Some claimed that inspections for booze would be intensified. Some talked about the deceased. He was serving a short sentence and had never gotten a leave. Eventually, the verdict was unanimously reached: "Fucking prison." In the darkest corners of their minds, they knew this could have happened to anyone. Each of us could have been in either pair of shoes. All knew the fault was with the prison. The pressure, the devastation, the abandonment, the loneliness, the hopelessness, the bad moment.

After all, it's one word: prison. Everyone knows eighteen years is a long time. They call it "too much prison" and it's articulated with a sigh. Everyone knows that in eighteen years you lose yourself, your hopes, your dreams, your liveliness, your dignity, your humanity—you lose all that makes you a human being. You get down to zero. Most felt lucky to have not been the cursed ones this time.

Two weeks later and it's the same old story, again. It's nine and they haven't let us out yet. I suffocate in the cell. Someone must have gotten stabbed again, I guess. At some point the guard comes and opens up. I get myself to the kitchen and put the kettle on. Before getting around to making my coffee, I get the news: Kostas hanged himself in solitary confinement.

10/11/2012

Concrete and iron.

Rain lets mountain scents settle upon concrete and iron.

A stormy havoc gives life to prison. This primeval hazard
  makes it a shelter.
Sometimes gloom plays a harp within my chest, spiking my
  tear ducts.
The 32 steps of the yard can't fit in my thoughts. I don't fit in
  the yard. I don't fit in prison.
A cage for humans. A cage for incapacitated outlaws.

On the other hand:

The sacred right to employment.
A worker's right to build a prison.
An electrician's to put up the security system.

An architect's to design it.

A guard's right.

Fuck this culture of capital.
Concrete and iron.

The prisoners are strong like concrete and iron.
Not like diamond.
Blessed are those imprisoned. No man can arrest them.
Blessed are those definitively sentenced. No man can
  convict them.

Greek prison dictionary

Phonetic script notes:

/θ/ as in <u>th</u>ink

/δ/ as in <u>th</u>ere

/γ/ as in <u>y</u>es before /i/ and /e/ but weaker before consonants and other vowels

/g/ as in <u>g</u>ap

/i/ as in b<u>i</u>t

/e/ as in p<u>e</u>t

/r/ like a tapped r, as often pronounced in Scotland

/a/ is somewhere between c<u>a</u>t and c<u>u</u>t

/o/ as in p<u>o</u>t with the lips slightly more rounded

/p/, /k/ and /t/ are always unaspirated and slightly stronger than in English

/h/ like the German 'ch' before /e/ and /i/ but like the Spanish "j" before everything else

All vowels are pronounced in strong forms, there's no "schwa" sound.

An apostrophe (') is marked before the stressed syllables.

Hopefully, readers won't find themselves in need of mastering Greek prison slang. But in the unfortunate case they do, pronunciation will be a minor issue in their life as prisoners in Greece.

Αγροτική (/aɣroti'ki/): farm prison. The farm prison is basically a stage the prisoner goes through before getting released and is consequently accompanied by feelings of salvation. It embodies an almost supernatural dimension in prison society. In most cases, the prisoner is transferred to a farm prison following an application he submits after he returns from his first leave. This process might take months as the first few applications are often rejected.

Farm prisons appeal to prisoners for various reasons, like the less-wretched living conditions. The primary reason, though, is the better labor days, which help suspension limits to be reached more quickly.

Prisoners undertake either agricultural and livestock farming activities or white-collar posts related to prison or production management.

New entrants to farm prisons reside in the "closed" part, meaning the chamber. After a certain period of time, they are transferred to the "open" part, namely the "houselets." As soon as a prisoner reaches this stage of semi-freedom with very loose invigilation, it's up to him to choose to escape or not, and therefore, he's referred to as a *"word-of-honor-er."*[22]

Farm prisons can be found in Kassandra of Halkidiki, Kasaveteia of Volos, Agia of Crete, Tirintha, and Avlonas.

Also, farm prisons host prisoners with short sentences or those charged with less serious offenses.

Άδεια (/'aδia/): leave. Perhaps the greatest decompression measure available in the Greek prison system. It was

---

22. See "Λογοτιμήτης (/loɣoti'mitis/)": "word-of-honor-er."

established—like all the favorable prison measures—in the nineties, following the prisoners' struggles.

A prisoner is entitled to a leave after he's covered one-fifth of his real sentence.[23] It's commonplace for leaves to be denied, especially in cases of long sentences. For example, in the case of life imprisonment, even if prisoners are entitled to a leave after the eighth year, the prison council tells them to be patient and that lifers are normally granted a leave after the tenth year.

The process towards the first leave—the following ones are considered regular—is soul-destroying for prisoners. Every two months they anticipate a pending council hearing, feeling overly hopeful, but they usually return full of gloom.

A prisoner who is on leave gets out for a few days—a maximum of nine—every two months. The days on leave cannot exceed a maximum of forty-five annually.

Returning from the first leave is usually not at all painful since the institutionalization makes the voluntary reentrance feel like a natural process. Life inside the prison feels more natural than outside of it. Getting accustomed, however, takes time.

The reentrance process is considerably degrading, since the prisoner has to spend a few days in the hole until he defecates in a bucket in the presence of a guard. The contents are then thoroughly examined to prevent any smuggling of small objects, or often, small amounts of drugs.

Αδίκημα (/a'ðikima/): offense. Prisoners tend to use the less journalistic and not-so-charged legal term "offense" instead of

---

23. As opposed to nominal. See "Σκαστά (/skas'ta/)": the nominal years of one's sentence, without counting the already served or to-be-served labor days in.

crime. The same logic applies when using the word homicide rather than murder.

Prisoners may also call one another *"serious offense"* as a declaration of respect.[24]

The offense one prisoner is charged with or is accused of is yet another parameter of the maze-like hierarchy system in prison. This, of course, correlates with the length of the corresponding sentence. Therefore, homicide comes with a higher index than migrant smuggling and a bank robber enjoys a higher index than a kiosk robber. The respect the bank robber enjoys, compared to that of the kiosk robber, has no class-based interpretations but mostly reflects the recognition of one's skills to live up to the demands of this offense.

The offense alone is by no means the only parameter that can ensure a higher place in the prison hierarchy.

Αδυναμία (/aδina'mia/): a fraggle (literally, a weakness). A denomination given to those in the lowest ranks of the prison hierarchy. It's commonly used in a pejorative way when referring to bullies, especially in the expression *"he's only mugging off the fraggles,"*[25] which sets out to accentuate their cowardice.

Ακούω (/a'kuo/): hear. The years of imprisonment one *"hears"* at court is the nominal sentence imposed, which—accounting for labor days as well as suspensions—ends up to actually amount to something less than half of this initial number. So, one who hears twenty-five years (thus, called a twenty-five-er)

---

24. σοβαρό αδίκημα (/sova'ro a'δikima/).
25. "μόνο με αδυναμίες τα βάζει" (/'mono me aδina'mies ta 'vazi/).

gauges to actually serve nine to twelve years and hopes to hear somewhat less at the Court of Appeal.

There's the expression "he heard years"[26] as opposed to "he heard life," meaning the accused escaped life imprisonment and his sentence was relatively milder.

Conversely, there's the expression "he heard it"[27] when one is sentenced to life imprisonment or when the sentence is considered unfair, too strict or longer than expected.

Ακρόαση (/a'kroasi/): hearing. It's the hearing request towards the head officer, the sergeant, the doctor or any other person whose name is found in the prison service organogram.

The prisoner slips an application inside a box placed in his wing and waits to be called in the following day. In the tightly controlled prison environment, every minor issue a prisoner might face needs to be solved with the sergeant's consent. The purpose of a sergeant's hearing may vary and could be about, for example, permission to have a flash drive, a request for an open visit—meaning without having a protective glass between you and your visitor—snitching on someone, a change of wing or participation in labor days, a visit to the library, permission to have a mechanical pencil, dental floss or any other object the prohibition of which is blatantly irrational.

No matter what problem a prisoner might encounter, the solution is always the expression "slip a hearing."[28] Prisoners

26. "άκουσε χρόνια" (/'akuse 'hronia) as opposed to "ακουσε ισόβια" (/'akuse i'sovia/).

27. "την άκουσε" (/tin 'akuse/).

28. "ρίξε ακρόαση" (/'rixe ak'roasi/).

who, for whatever reason, enjoy a higher status do not slip hearings, but simply ask the guard at the wing's gate—or the watch point, depending on the prison—to forward his request to the front or upper desk—again this varies from prison to prison. The front or upper desk is the sergeant's office. Not much later, the prisoner is called into his office without having filed an application beforehand.

Also, there's a hearing from the prison governor, this elusive figure, who negotiates what the sergeant refuses to take responsibility for. Then there's the hearing from the registrars or the accountants. The former cater to bureaucratic matters while the latter to the prisoners' personal accounts and possible undue charges and subsequent corrections.

In prisons that employ social workers, one can apparently slip a hearing for them too. The purpose is primarily to get a visit permission granted. However, in reality their role is mostly decorative.

If the prisoner needs medical attention, he slips a hearing for the doctor and if he's lucky and persistent enough, the doctor might call him—hopefully before it's too late.

Ακτίνα (/ak'tina/): block (see "πτέρυγα").

Αλητομπερδεμένος (/alitoberδe'menos/): trouble-meddler. Compound word with self-explanatory meaning. It's the prisoner who's involved in dark and shady business.

Αλομπερτίνα (/aloper'din/): Aloperidin, a very strong psych drug. It works almost like a lobotomy and is administered chiefly for disciplinary purposes. Even months after its administration, the prisoner is in mental and physical suppression. He can't move or speak and is highly likely to have suffered permanent damage.

Ανακοινώσεις (/anaki'nosis/): announcements. Announcements are made during the time the prison remains open. They might have to do with various issues. For instance, a prisoner can be called in to go to the wing's gate or the watch point for personal matters. These may range from collecting a letter or check—when the postman arrives—to having a visitor or a hearing from the sergeant or the prison governor. Also, whatever relates to a prisoner's daily life, say an upcoming water outage or the grocer's arrival or the opening of the canteen and so on, is promulgated by prison staff in the form of announcements on the speakers.

Ανήλικα (/a'nilika/): minors. The juvenile hall. There's the expression "when I was in minors,"[29] meaning when I was in the juvenile hall. The two main juvenile halls are in Avlonas and Kassavetia of Volos. Therefore, those prisoners are called "*kassavetia.*"

The juvenile halls are the cruelest of all prisons. Not so much because of the prison service but rather the "material."[30]

It's easy to tell whether one has served in the minors. The trait that singles them out is the way they play their worry beads, passing it through all their fingers very quickly. If the worry beads fall off one's hands, the guy who'll pick it up and hand it back to the owner declares their submission and that's why it's

29. "Όταν ήμουν στα ανήλικα" (/'otan 'imun sta a'nilika/).
30. See "Υλικό (/ili'ko/)": material.

considered a test of submissiveness for freshmen. If a prisoner wishes to appear polite but skips all these rituals, then they simply leave it next to the owner—not in the owner's hands—after giving it a round through his fingers first.

Another typical feature of those who've served in minors is the tattoo of the saint. It's a stick man with a halo just like a toddler's drawing: a circle for the head, a vertical line for the body, a horizontal line for hands and an inverted V for legs. Another horizontal line above the head makes the halo. This small tattoo is chiefly found on a finger or toe and is supposed to symbolize the saint of the outlaws.

Ανοιχτή φυλακή (/anih'ti fila'ki/): open prison. The prison remains open from 8 a.m. to 12 p.m. and then from 3 p.m. to 8 p.m. Open prison means the doors of the cells remain open, allowing prisoners to roam about from cell to cell within the wing. Most activities like working out, cooking, sports, and board games are conducted in open prison.

The open prison time isn't the same as the yard time. The latter varies from prison to prison but, in all cases, it is shorter than the open prison time. For instance, the yard closes one hour before sunset in all prisons; consequently, the yard time and open prison time only happen to coincide during a few summer months.

Άπιαστα (/'apiasta/): uncaught. It's a word predominantly used in drug-related cases. When an amount of drugs has not been confiscated and remains unfound but its existence and dealing has been confirmed by means of tapped phones, police officers' testimonies or a co-respondent's confession, then this amount—most likely a number of kilos—is called "uncaught."

The uncaught usually comes with a milder sentence since, according to the invariable tactics of the Greek penal system, whoever is accused without sufficient evidence is considered "less guilty" rather than innocent.

The word has inherited a broader meaning and is now used in other cases beyond drug trafficking. It refers to ungrounded or evidence-lacking arrests.

Αποχή συσσιτίου (/apo'hi sisi'tiu/): ration abstinence. It's a form of symbolic protest different from a hunger strike in that prisoners refuse to collect the prison food, meaning their ration. They still eat what they buy from the canteen or the grocer.

When ration abstinence is conducted on a large scale, it ends up to be merely a manifestation of class-based contrasts, given that prisoners don't enjoy the same purchasing power. As a result, most feed on rice and bread only while others suffer no shortages whatsoever.

Αρνητικός (/arniti'kos/): negative. It's the accused who denies all accusations. There's the expression "he goes negative"[31] (meaning to court). It is considered honorable to have gone negative since it means one endured the torment of interrogation and, therefore, it is guaranteed he is not a grass. The prisoners don't really care if the accusations hold true or not, assuming

31. "πάει αρνητικός" (/'pai arniti'kos/).

that even if you haven't done what you're accused of, then certainly you've done something else.

Αρσενικός (/arseni'kos): manly. A word commonly used to describe a prisoner's fair, straightforward or even non-submissive personality.

Αρχιφύλακας (/arhi'filakas/): sergeant. The sergeant is entrusted with the prison's administration, chiefly the practical matters, and can be contrasted to the governor, whose job is mainly bureaucratic. Between their roles, there's an analogy similar to that between a prime minister and a president. In some prisons—depending on the prison's tradition and the individuals' personalities—it's only one of the two who is the actual boss. As a result, the governor's role is decorative, despite the higher ranking.

The prison's administration involves the line management and supervision of the guards as well as the regulation of all prisoners' lives. Each sergeant coins his own methods but, to an extent, they're restricted by the special circumstances and subsequent traditions of each prison. For example, if a prison is traditionally controlled with dope and its trafficking, which keeps the population suppressed and simultaneously brings some profit to hierarchically senior prisoners in exchange for their service to ensure social peace within the prison, then the sergeant cannot stop it, no matter how strong his will may be.

The sergeant's post requires special skills, from processing and systemizing methods and applications of control to deploying new practices that are tailor-made for each individual prisoner. Managing and keeping hundreds of confined people in relative peace is a science. Within the absolutely systemized context of prison, each prisoner needs special treatment if peace is to be maintained. The recipe is fear or violence for the weaker ones, especially those who are isolated from families or the prison society, and additional privileges for the more assertive, wealthier or socially and financially connected prisoners. Moreover, the sergeant is called in to handle conflicts among guards as well as the vendettas and clashes of interests among prisoners.

Everything goes through the sergeant's hands. He has to get guards and grasses to keep him well informed about even the slightest change in every prisoner's behavior.

Αρχιφυλακεύων (/arhifila'kevon/): senior sub-sergeant, the first in command among the ranks of sub-sergeants. He's the sergeant's successor and therefore the one in charge when the sergeant is absent.

Ατλακόλ (/atla'kol/): Atlacoll is a white, hydro-soluble, stucco-like glue used widely in Greek prisons. It's absolutely indispensable when it comes to all sorts of crafts, from sticking bed sheets onto walls, to framing and hanging handmade carton shelves or hangers made of wooden cloth-pegs, to making DIY weights. Unlike other kinds of glue, such as instant glue, Atlacoll is available without the sergeant's permission.

Βαπόρι (/va'pori/): pusher; literally, steamboat. This title is awarded to guards who provide prisoners with forbidden goods, like mobile phones or drugs, in exchange for a certain amount of money. Depending on the number of pushers in each prison or the ease with which they push their goods, the prices may fluctuate, following the laws of supply and demand. Adding up all the transactions, the aggregate amount of money given to pushers within a prison is astronomical.

Βάρη (/'vari/): weights. These are the handmade weights that prisoners use in their workouts. Except for a few blocks in certain prisons, metal weights are forbidden. Prisoners are particularly inventive and resourceful when it comes to turning whatever kind of metal object into a weapon, thus prison service limits the metal objects permitted down to the absolutely necessary ones, like pots, pans, etc.

Prisoners make their own weights by filling up some plastic bottles—their number and size (half or one liter) varies, depending on the intended overall weight—with salt and water and tying them together using strips of bed sheets soaked in Atlacoll. If they want to make a durable bar, they strap them on the ends of three broomsticks that are tied together with bed-sheet strips and Atlacoll. If they want to make dumbbells, they clamp them on a small piece of broomstick.

Βράζω (/'vrazo/): literally, to boil. Figuratively, to distill, make booze.

Γενική (/γeni'ki/): literally, general. It's the general cleaning of the cell. Normally, it's scheduled for once a week or even more frequently. The residents or the *housewives*[32] of the cell or block remove all possessions and furniture—bags with clothes,

32. See "Λεγκένης (/le'genis/)": prison wife.

plastic tables, shoes, slippers, plastic wheeled fruit-storage boxes, plastic stools, cartons, etc.—from the cell, pour water with a bucket along with lots of floor-cleaning products (combined with clothes detergent to make foam), and rub with the broom. Then, they sweep up the water with the "dry"[33] [the squeegee], leading it to the floor drain and, finally, wait until the floor dries up before dusting and putting all their stuff back in.

Γράμμα (/'γrama/): letter. Since there is no Internet access, and given the outrageous cost of trunk calls coupled with the quirky existential state prisoners find themselves in, traditional mail still flourishes in Greek prisons. The ardor and intensity prisoners experience in anticipation of a letter reminds one of romance novels from bygone eras.

Γράφω/ Έγραψα (/'γrafo/ 'εγrapsa/): write/wrote. Words used when saying that a prisoner has placed an order at the prison's canteen or the grocer's; the latter is outside the prison.

Διευθυντής (/δiefθi'dis/): governor.[34] He's the highest in the ranks among prison personnel and is normally in charge of bureaucratic matters and has no personal involvement in managing the prisoners.

The governor's office is housed separately in the prison, usually with other bureaucratic offices. The interior design of this place, with its luxurious desk, bears no resemblance to a prison

33. See "Στεγνή (steγ'ni/)": literally, dry; figuratively, squeegee.
34. Compare with sergeant ("αρχιφύλακας").

environment. The sergeant's office, on the other hand, looks clearly and noticeably like part of the prison.

If we draw parallels between the prison and Plato's society, then the governor and the civil servants surrounding him are the golden society, the sergeant and the guards are the silver, and the prisoners are the iron.

Δίζυγο (/'ðiziɣo/): parallel bars. It's perhaps the most popular workout equipment alongside pull-up bars. In reality, it's a cheap handicraft made of two hollow iron tubes that form right angles. One end is bolted on the wall and the other is secured to the floor.

Prisoners use the parallel bars for a variety of exercises such as pull-ups for the chest and triceps as well as leg lifts to strengthen the lower abdominals.

Διπλή (/ðip'li/): literally, double. It's the "double line," the way prisoners from different prisons communicate. It's an invaluable service for the prisoners' communication. Two to five prisoners from different prisons call a certain number at an arranged time and the owner of the number who lives "in the out" mediates.[35] The mediators are generally friends or relatives of a prisoner who take part in the communication process. This service is usually offered in exchange for money. If a prisoner wishes to have regular access to a "double" they have to pay a monthly fee.

Εικοσιπεντάρης (/ikosipe'ðaris/): twenty-fiver. It's the prisoner whose sentence is at least twenty-five years but not life

---

35. The phrase "in the out" means in society, outside prison.

imprisonment. In the Greek penal system all sentences beyond life imprisonment, meaning more than twenty-five, are reduced to twenty-five years. So, one whose final sentence might be twenty-five, twenty-six, twenty-seven, or even five-hundred years is entitled to a sentence suspension once he's served three-fifths of the twenty-five years, which is fifteen years in aggregate (counting actual prison time as well as labor days). A twenty-fiver serves an average of nine to twelve years and is the second in rank among the long-term convicts, following the lifer.

Εικοσιτεσσάρης(/ikosite'saris/): twenty-fourer. He's the prisoner who makes use of the favorable Article 24 chiefly in drug-related cases.[36] He grasses on other people and gives facts to the police not only about his own case but also other cases he might be aware of, in order to enjoy a more lenient treatment at court. The twenty-fourer is considered the most disgraceful of all kinds of grasses.

Επισκεπτήριο (/episkep'tirio/): visiting hours. The visiting system varies from prison to prison. It may vary in terms of the time allowed, the frequency, as well as the visitors' relation to the prisoner (it can be restricted to family only or expanded to friends, as well). Moreover, each prison decides independently if the visits are "free"—also known as "open"—meaning without the intrusive protective glass.

Visits constitute an integral but painstaking process in a prisoner's life since he meets his loved ones under conditions

36. Article 24 (Law 1729/87), titled "Repentance," states that if a perpetrator became a criminal informant the court might order a reprieve of the execution of their sentence.

that are not pleasant at all, especially due to the strict invigilation, the often overtly indiscreet presence of the guards, the protective glass and the limited time.

The visits are the prisoner's only chance to get hold of clothes, cushions, bed sheets, shoes, books or any other object that he might be permitted to possess but can't be found at the prison's canteen or grocery shop.

Επιταγή (/epita'γi/): check. The only way a prisoner can get money in his account is to either have a visitor deposit it at the prison's accounting office or have someone send a postal money order.

Just like letters, checks might take some days to be delivered, which can be soul-destroying for the prisoner as he's rendered incapable of placing his weekly order to the canteen or the grocer's and is thus unable to cover his basic needs for several weeks.

The postman delivers the invoice which references the amount of money credited to the prisoner's account, not the actual money, of course, since possessing money is prohibited.

Εργόχειρα (/er'γohira/): handicrafts. Some prisoners make handicrafts in order to either secure an income or spend their time creatively. Most of the time, they use simple materials such as wooden sticks or beads or even the soft bit of bread mixed with Atlacoll.

The most common handicrafts are lighter cases and charms. With very few exceptions, and despite the whatever know-how and patience their crafting takes, these handicrafts are monuments of tackiness.

They are sold in bazaars organized by charities or to monasteries or even to other prisoners.

Έρευνα (/'erevna/): investigation. Refers to two sorts of investigation.

First, there's the reception investigation, administered to newcomers, to those transferred as well as those returning from court, the hospital or a leave. In these cases, the prisoner undergoes meticulous scrutiny. For starters, he takes all his clothes off. Then, he is coerced into a humiliating procedure called "squat and cough," which means he squats deeply and coughs. This is to examine if one's "tucked"[37] any prohibited objects. All of his belongings are searched too, especially luggage with clothes.

The second kind of investigation is that of the cell. This is conducted in closed prison and, needless to say, without warning. It can be ordered by the guards—and thus be considered regular—or by a public prosecutor. The former is conducted by the guards in the presence of the sub-sergeant while the latter by a public prosecutor in the presence of the governor as well the rather indiscreet Special Suppressive Counter-Terrorism Unit.

Εφετείο (/efe'tio/): Court of Appeal. Prisoners are in the same anticipation of the Court of Appeal as the Christians are of Christ's Second Coming. Usually, the Court of Appeal does justice by putting the sentence into its right dimensions or acquitting the prisoner. This anticipation, tapped with hopes for reduction, is part of the prisoners' punishment in the medieval

37. Hide in one's anus. See "Λουκαδώρος—Λουκάρω (/luka'ðoros—lu'karo/)": tucker—or, to tuck.

Greek penal system, since, in practice, the prisoner spends years serving a sentence greatly incommensurate to the crime he committed.

In Greece, a trial at a Court of Appeal can take from two to ten years, counting from the initial sentence to the new verdict. Until then, the prisoner just waits.

Generally, the conclusion is that from all stages of criminal justice, the one and only thing prisoners have some faith in is the Court of Appeal.

Θάλαμος (/'θalamos/): chamber. Prisons may comprise cells, chambers or a mixture of both. The chamber can host from eight to twenty people who are made to share the room, toilet, and bathroom as well as one another's quirks of daily life. Life in the chamber is very harsh and soul-destroying for prisoners.

Θαμνάκιας (/θam'nakias/): bushman, meaning a hitman.

Θηλιά (/θili'a/): hitch. The prisoner twines a hitch when he intends to hang himself. It's normally braided strips of bed-sheet cloth made durable enough to bear their weight. When a prisoner is desperate and tells others "I'll twine the hitch,"[38] implying that he means to hang himself, the others reply "the soap is on me"[39] or "let me kick the footstool for you."[40] When, in desperation, a prisoner tells a guard he'll "twine the hitch," the guard's reply is invariably "don't dare threaten me."

---

38. "Θα βάλω θηλιά" (/θa 'valo θili'a/).

39. "Το σαπούνι στο βάζω εγώ" (/to sa'puni sto 'vazo e'γo).

40. "Το σκαμνί θα στο κλωτσήσω εγώ" (/to skam'ni θa sto klo'tsiso e'γo/).

I believe these replies are perfectly appropriate and aim to disperse thoughts of this sort rather than exacerbate them with cruelty.

Ιεραρχία (/ierar'hia/): hierarchy. Hierarchical division is very intense in prison. It's a very intricate, maze-like, and multifaceted system. There's no standard trait that places a prisoner higher or lower in the hierarchy. Instead, there are traits in combination that give each prisoner a place in the interrelated prison regime. Some of these are the prisoner's connections to the black market outside prison, his sentence, the crime he committed, his level of mastery in martial arts, his indifference towards disciplinary or penal consequences, his race, his financial prominence, his network or his inveteracy.

For example, there's an unquestionable respect for long-termers or veteran prisoners—meaning more than fifteen years in prison—as an earnest recognition of the difficulties they've faced or will face due to their long sentences. The same applies for the kind of crime, there's a different index of respect for a bank robber and a bag snatcher. The race a prisoner belongs to plays a major role. Not only does each race have its own internal hierarchy, race itself can designate a prisoner's place within the general system of hierarchy. For instance, Greeks, Albanians, and Russians enjoy higher rankings if compared to Pakistanis, Gypsies or Blacks. In between, there are the Arabs and Kurds. The Russians are the sole group characterized by a cemented and systemized internal hierarchy.

Prison service values this hierarchy and actually promotes a system of hierarchical representation, which helps them manage the prison more effectively. Following the example of the Ottoman Empire, they assign the task of best management practice to the leaders of each race or block and allow some privileges in exchange. So, in a way, the power to negotiate with the service and the level of influence on other prisoners are two fundamentally interrelated aspects that affect one another and thus define one's place in the prison hierarchy.

The social status one may enjoy inside prison rarely corresponds to that on the outside.

The prisoner who's hierarchically on the top of each block is called—with an inkling of class-based sarcasm—"president," "boss," "big" or "chief."[41] Lower in the hierarchy one finds the "taxis," the "prison wives," and the "fraggles."[42]

Hierarchy may sometimes differ from block to block in order to adjust to the related "material."[43] As a result, depending on the power pendulum, two prisoners with identical traits might take reverse places in different blocks.

In the closed prison environment it's blatantly obvious that justice hinges entirely on power. While there's a common notion of fairness, recognition of power and hierarchical norms backs it down.

The level of Byzantinism and scheming in the battle for a move up in the prison hierarchy is even more repulsive than that found on the political scene.

---

41. "πρόεδρος" (/ 'proeðros/), "αφεντικό" (/afedi'ko/), "μεγάλος" (/me'γalos/) or "αρχηγός" (/arhi'gos/).

42. See respectively "Ταξί (/ta'xi/)": literally, taxi; "Λεγκένης (/le'genis/)": prison wife; "Αδυναμία (/aðina'mia/)": a fraggle (literally, a weakness).

43. See "Υλικό (/ili'ko/)": material.

Ισοβίτης (/iso'vitis/): lifer; the prisoner who's been convicted to life imprisonment. The term usually refers to those who have already heard their final verdict, meaning those who didn't manage to get their sentence reduced at the Court of Appeal.

The longest someone can serve in prison is twenty-five years. Consequently, if one's sentence is life imprisonment, they must serve a twenty-five–year mixed sentence, which is much longer than a life, or ask for suspension as soon as he completes four-fifths of his mixed sentence—instead of the three-fifths that normally applies in other sentences. The mixed sentence is estimated with the labor days taken into account. As regards labor days, a lifer is entitled to a maximum of four years, therefore, he must serve sixteen years of actual imprisonment.

Also, there are nominally longer sentences like life imprisonment *plus*, double or triple life imprisonment or even more. In this case, after the sixteenth year, the prisoner must serve two-fifths of the remaining sentence. In essence, the penal system grants discounts to big numbers only. In any case, the suspension limit is the twenty-first year while the upper limit of continuous confinement is twenty-five years.

The lifer usually enjoys a greater degree of respect. On the one hand, this stems from the recognition of the hardships he's been through or will be going through. On the other, it's the fact that he has nothing to lose and this makes him dangerous in the suffocating prison environment.

Even those who fervently advocate that prisons must exist ought to regard every sentence that makes an individual spend more than five years in confinement as perverse sadism.

Καζάνι (/ka'zani/): cauldron.

(1) Legume soup or any other sort of soupy food. The term is attributed to the big cauldrons used in the preparation of prison food.

(2) A welfare policy norm followed by Russian prisoners. Part of each prisoner's orders placed at the canteen or grocer's—mainly cigarettes and phone credit—end up in the cauldron. If a member of this community has no money in his account then he can borrow from the cauldron. Part of the profit made in gambling ends up in the cauldron. However, borrowing from the cauldron to gamble or buy drugs is strictly prohibited.

Καθαριστής (/kaθari'stis/): cleaner. It's the most common form of prison labor. Under the command of the head cleaner, cleaners are let out when prison is closed and clean the block. Some prisoners consider this post degrading and they either pay someone else monthly in tobacco to do the work on their behalf or don't bother to get out of their cells whatsoever. Another reason that the cleaner's post is not highly revered stems from its temporality, which follows a three-month rotation.

The head cleaner's post, on the other hand, is different since it's permanent and is normally undertaken by prisoners who are high in the block's hierarchy. As a rule, the head cleaner represents the block before the prison staff and attends to any technical or everyday-life–related problems that are forever arising.

Κάθειρξη (/'kaθirksi/): there's no corresponding legal term in English, so we'll simply call it "*kathirksi.*"

The difference between common imprisonment and kathirksi is the time prisoners need to have served before reaching their suspension limit. Kathirksi requires three-fifths of the length of the mixed sentence when the equivalent for common imprisonment is two-fifths. Sentences from one to five years can only be considered common imprisonment, five to ten can be either common or kathirksi, while more than ten years can only be kathirksi.

Καλαμάκια (/kala'makia/): sticks. They're the wooden kebab sticks that are very often used in handicraft creations like lighter cases, tobacco cases, shelves, coffee tables, etc.

Καντίνα (/ka'dina/): canteen. The canteen provides prisoners with basic consumer staples such as phone cards, cigarettes, tobacco, envelopes with prepaid stamps, coffee, toilet paper, bottled water, lighters, mail paper, sugar, cookies, pens, oil, rice, pasta. In some prisons, to purchase one must place an order and this happens twice a week. In others, there's a permanent canteen or there's a trolley that passes daily, in which case transactions are made with tokens. The canteen and the grocer's are two different things.

Καντινιέρης (/kadini'eris/): canteen-man. It's a labor post that involves a prisoner taking notes of the other prisoners' orders and distributing the goods both from the canteen and the grocer's. The inspection and accounting is a guard's responsibility.

Καπάκι (/ka'paki/): bottle top. It's a unit of measurement for drugs, given the lack of scales or other reliable measuring instruments. In prison dope is not sold by the gram but by crystal Bic pen caps. It's usually cut with Depon[44] tablets. The unit of measurement for weed is the top of big water bottles.

Κάπνος (/kap'nos/): tobacco pouch. Given their financial constraints, the majority of prisoners smoke roll-ups rather than cigarettes. Tobacco as well as phone cards are widely used in the barter economy.

Καρατέκα (/kara'teka/): *karateka* is an archaic expression, albeit still present in Greek prisons, referring to knowledge of martial arts other than wrestling.

Κάρτα (/'karta/): card.
(1) When one prisoner "has got a card with"[45] another prisoner, this means they have unsettled business.

(2) The phone card: It can be a ten or fourteen-euro one. Beyond its conventional use, it can also be traded when money comes short.

Καρτοτηλέφωνο (/kartoti'lefono/): a public payphone. One of the victories won after the bloody prisoner uprisings of the nineties. Before, if a prisoner wished to contact his relatives, he would "slip a hearing" and the call would take place in the sergeant's office. The sergeant openly invigilated the call using another headset.

Nowadays, public payphones constitute the main medium of communication with society. The use of mobile phones is

---

44. Depon is a common over-the-counter analgesic found in Greece. It's equivalent to Paracetamol in the UK or Tylenol in North America.

45. "έχει κάρτα με. . ." (/'ehi 'karta me . . . /).

relatively widespread, but in some places, given that their possession is prohibited, mobile phones are luxury goods.

Κατσαρίδες (/katsa'riðes/): cockroaches. They're a plague in most Greek prisons. In Korydallos their number is so large that you see them walking on pillows or even appearing in between the digits on the payphone screens, which make a hospitable nesting environment just like all devices do; they're like pet containers.

Κελί (/ke'li/): cell. Prisoners either live in cells or chambers. Within the cell or chamber stands the one and only private space a prisoner enjoys: his bed. Depending on the prison, the block, and the prisoner, cells vary in terms of capacity and go from single cells—rather rare—to five-bed cells, which pay no respect whatsoever to notions of dignity. The "norm" is for a cell to host two to three prisoners.

The cell is where the prisoner has to spend at least fifteen hours per day, so whether his days will be bearable or not depends heavily on the mix of cellmates.

By default, a cell comes with beds, a plastic table, and a plastic chair. Prisoners make any additional furniture by creating various patents. For example, curtains for the window or the entrance are made of bed sheets. Likewise, curtains are made for around the bed to grant some privacy. To make wall hangers, prisoners usually use wooden clothespins attached to the wall with Atlacoll. To make shelves, they use cardboard also stuck together with Atlacoll.

The walls of the cell are frequently coated with blankets around the bed area to absorb humidity. Bed sheets may also be scattered over the rest of the surfaces to add some color while country or football club flags mark each prisoner's identity. It's not uncommon to see a Che Guevara or a Spiderman poster, a bed sheet with teddy bears and moons, a Greek flag, and an AEK football club flag all together in a row.

Decoration varies from cell to cell depending on tastes, artistry, mix of people, and the dwellers' economic means. Practicality prevails over aesthetics.

Depending on the prison, cells might include a private bathroom and hot water. For example, in new prisons one can find a toilet with a door. In Korydallos prison showers are shared and located in the basement while the toilets are inside the cells and separated from the rest of the room with plasterboard and a DIY folding screen. When a prisoner wishes to poo, he makes sure to do so before the prison gets closed. He asks his cellmates to leave the cell and hangs a warning sign on the cell door with the indication "W.C."

Κιγκλίδα (/kig'lida/): the entrance to an old prison block, which has nowadays given its place to the watch point. It's an iron-barred gate where the guard spends his shift and the prisoner runs to when he needs something from the prison service or when others are after him to lynch him.

Κιούπι (/ki'upi/): the hole [literally, a clay pot]. This term means either the disciplinary cell or the freshman's cell. In the former case, it refers to a disciplinary punishment also known as solitary confinement or guardhouse. In the latter, it's the separate rooms where prisoners are kept temporarily when transferred from prison to prison or when coming back from a leave and are thus suspected of having abused illegal substances or swallowed small amounts of them with a view to "drilling the prison."[46] During their stay, in the latter case, prisoners must squat and cough.

Κλειστή φυλακή (/klis'ti fyla'ki/): closed prison.
(1) It's the prison which is not a court prison, meaning not for those simply prosecuted and detained—but convicted instead—like Korydallos, Ioannina, Komotini or Amfisa prisons. Or, the prison which is not a farm prison. These host prisoners with short sentences or prisoners who have reached the final stage of their sentence. Closed prisons are different from court or farm prisons in that control over prisoners' lives is tighter.

(2) A prison is considered closed for as long as the prisoners are locked down in their cells. The prison remains closed for fifteen hours per day: from 8 p.m. to 8 a.m. and from 12 a.m. to 3 p.m.

Κλέφτης ('kleftis/): literally, thief. Also, a prison-made electronic device used to boil liquids, notably one that resembles wine and is later distilled to booze.[47] It's a piece of wire—usually removed from a fan or radio—bearing a plug on one end and on the other are two pieces of iron attached onto each stripline. The iron is usually taken from a grill or water drain cover. When the DIY device is plugged in and the iron end is dipped in a plastic bucket full of liquid, the liquid starts to warm and eventually boils.

46. See "Τρυπάω (/tri'pao/)": drill.
47. See "Τσίπουρο (/'tsipuro/)": brew.

Κοινωνία (/kino'nia/): the out [literally, society]. There's the expression "when I was in the out," meaning when I was out of prison. Likewise, refers to an object obtained outside the prison; prisoners say they bought it in the out. When one gets hold of a bottle of proper liquor, as opposed to prison-made booze, then this is called "κοινωνίτικο" (/kino'nitiko/) [societal].

Κόκκινοι (/'kokini/): reds. An archaic nickname attributed to Russian prisoners.

Κομοδίνο (/komo'ðino/): literally, bedside table. A term used to describe a prisoner who has suffered a chemical lobotomy—usually as a disciplinary measure—resulting in temporary or permanent loss of consciousness. The drug used to this end is Aloperidin.[48] The prisoner who returns from a prison's psychiatric clinic back to his block is like a vegetable.

The term is widely used to describe the naïve, the half-insane, and prisoners of limited intellect.

Κοριοί (/Kor'γi/): bed bugs. They are a plague in many Greek prisons.

Κοτέτσι (/ko'tetsi/): literally, chicken coop. Another term for the court prisons, which are most of the time small and their conditions remind you of barns. They're full of bed bugs, there's a noticeable shortage in space and beds so prisoners may sleep on the floor of the corridors, and sanitary conditions are far below the expected standards. More often than not, they're premises that

48. See "Αλομπερτίνα (/aloper'din/)": Aloperidin, a very strong psych drug.

weren't designed to serve as prisons. A striking example is that of Ioannina prison, which was initially a slaughterhouse, then a school, and finally was turned into prison. Ioannina and Amfissa prisons are the most infamous chicken coops in Greece.

Κουβέρτα (/ku'verta/): blanket. A blanket can be used in many different ways in prison. Beyond the classic use as a cover in wintertime, it's used as wall coat to absorb humidity and also as a work-out mat. Pieces of blanket can be used as welcome mats at the entrance of the cell. An additional way in which a blanket can come in handy is when carrying a dead body or a heavily injured prisoner who has been lynched, got into fight, committed suicide, overdosed, or more rarely, died by natural causes. The body is delivered to the watch point for further action.

Κούφια (/'kufia/): literally, hollow. It's the sentence or verdict at the Court of First Instance. It's usually absurdly strict or ungrounded even by the standards of Greece's third-world penal system. The prisoner is sure that the Court of Appeal will take remedial action. The term usually refers to "kathirksi" imprisonment[49] which usually—especially in drug cases—drops down to four years imprisonment.

Κωλοδάχτυλο (/kolo'ðahtilo/): assfinger. It's a term used in various expressions. For example, to voice desperation or warn people of your bad condition, you can use expressions such as "I'll assfinger myself" or "I'll kill myself with two assfingers" or three or four, depending on the seriousness of the case. There's

49. "κάθειρξη."

the expression " [go] assfinger yourself," which is presented as a solution to any problem a prisoner might complain about. It's also used as an excuse when someone occupies the toilet for too long. The following exchange is far from rare:

"Come on! What has he been up to?"
"Assfingering himself."

Λεγκένης (/le'genis/): prison wife. It's what the Albanians call the cleaner. It refers to a prisoner who's very low in the prison hierarchy. "*Legenis*" or "*legeni*" [masculine and neutral noun form, respectively] is coerced into the role of the servant either by means of threats of or actual violence. He does the laundry, cleans cells, makes coffee, cooks, and rolls tobacco. A thug will often take a legeni in his cell and have him at his exclusive service around the clock, while in other cases, a legeni offers his service to more than one prisoner irrespective of cohabitation.

Legenis differs from a "taxi" in that his service is free of charge.[50]

Λεχώνα (/le'hona/): literally, a woman who's recently given birth. It's a term to describe a prisoner who lies in his bed all day.

Λογοτιμήτης (/loɣoti'mitis/): "word-of-honor-er." A farm prisoner who is at the last stage of his sentence and lives in a state of semi-freedom. In essence, it means he's given his word of honor that he won't escape.

50. Greek prisons are homophobic and macho-friendly environments. The freer translation "prison wife" is used to denote the social stereotype of a housewife who contributes her unpaid labor towards the management of the household, but does not imply sexual relations, which constitutes a taboo that is not socially tolerated in Greek prisons.

Λουκαδώρος—Λουκάρω (/luka'δoros—lu'karo/): tucker—or, to tuck. It's a "drilling"[51] method. See "Κιούπι (/ki'upi/)": the hole [literally, a clay pot]. Tucking means hiding objects in one's anus—these could be small amounts of drugs—and comes in handy during prison transfers. Of course, it's not the only way to get things into prison and is definitely not the most effective, given that most of the time prisoners are subject to a squat and cough.[52] If the tucker passes the inspection successfully, what comes next is called "un-tucking." This means his co-prisoners give him a douche by inserting a hose in his anus. If the tucker has drilled large amounts of drugs, then he's called "luggage."[53]

Μαχαίρι (/ma'heri/): knife. Prison-made knives are very often masterpieces of folk art. They're made with materials found in abundance inside prison, like pieces of iron removed from whatever kind of source like windows or beds. They're sculpted with sandpaper and patience until they get the intended shape and, quite commonly, they bear sophisticated curves and hollows. The handle is normally less sophisticated and made of fabric or thick card-paper pieces due to shortages in other materials. Sometimes, though rarely, it might be coated with leather taken from a belt.

There are, of course, sloppily made knives as well. A simply sharpened blade will do the job. Collections of prison-made knives can be found in every sergeant's office, where they're normally kept in a big jar after having been confiscated during

51. See "Τρυπάω (/tri'pao/)": drill.
52. See "Έρευνα (/'erevna/)": investigation.
53. "μπαγκαζιέρα (/bagazi'era/).

inspections. They are displayed there in this medieval style as a reminder of the guards' authority over the prisoners.

Moreover, there are the small handmade knives, which are tolerated by prison service as they're only good for chopping vegetables and can cause no harm. They comprise a small blade—normally removed from a coffee pot or a floor-water drainer—and a handle made of the upper part of a toothbrush, a plastic utensil or a camping knife. After chiseling the plastic with the help of a lighter it's attached to the end of the blade.

Μεροκάματο (/mero'kamato/):
(1) Labor day. It's the favorable equivalence of one's sentence in unpaid working days. The prisoner undertakes the responsibility of a scheduled task and reduces his sentence by accumulating working months. A labor day can be of three types, namely 23, 30, and 45. One working month reduces the sentence by 23, 30, or 45 days, respectively. The most common labor day is 23 while the 45s are normally found in farm prisons.

There are many different working posts such as the head cleaner, cleaner, canteen-man, waiter, paramedic, librarian, the posts at the laundry or the guards' canteen, plumber, painter, repairman, etc. In some posts the work is like a token—symbolic—while in others it's proper work. The post is not usually decided upon by the prisoner himself but by his place in the prison's hierarchy.

The working posts, which make up a far smaller number than that of the prisoners, are assigned in a way that turns them into privilege. It's an important card in the service's sleeve, since the prisoner has to waive other entitlements in order to preserve his working post.

(2) When a wealthy but naïve prisoner—or one who's too weak to endure the prison environment—becomes a victim of fraud or psychological pressure, this results in him getting ripped off—his money, tobacco, phone cards—thus he's called "*μεροκάματο*." The ways in which one can become *μεροκάματο* are numerous. The basic ones, however, include being consistently and systematically robbed in card games or being provided protection, which means you're being offered protection by someone who would otherwise do you harm.

Μετανάστες (/meta'nastes/): migrants. The crime of human trafficking is called "migrants." In recent years there's been a sudden increase in the number of cases of this type and these prisoners, who are faced with unimaginable sentences, are migrants themselves. The circles of this kind found either in prison or on the black market deserve no respect.

Μοναστήρια (/monas'tiria/): monasteries.
(1) As with all asylums (hospitals, army camps, universities) that involve voluntary or imposed, temporary or permanent social exclusion, so with prisons. We can trace the origins of the prison back to the monasteries of feudal Europe, where marginalized and persecuted individuals found custodial confinement. Church and monastery prisons operated in the seventeenth century and provided protective confinement to various categories of unwanted individuals. It was during this era the theoretical foundation and basis for correctional imprisonment operations were developed.

Church and monastery prisons were created to facilitate and respond to the needs of those subjects of power who were in search of a sacred asylum from the oppressive mechanisms of feudal power. This pursuit made the church create special prisons near the sacred sites to provide custodial confinement to the persecuted.

Every individual who appeared themselves before any church service was subject to confession before being granted pardon, and then vowed his absolute submission to the church's abbot before God in order to enjoy this asylum-like protection provided by the church.

Prisoners were subjected to abasement and humiliation meant to trigger deep reflection and personal devastation, which in turn would lead to repentance and correction.

In the eighteenth century, the religious founders of corrective science and reformers of the punitive system (Cesare Beccaria, Jeremy Bentham, and John Howard) based their views on this monastic system. Nowadays, the structure, operation, schedule and terminology of prisons resemble those of monasteries to a great extent. You see social disintegration and exclusion from society, a strict schedule, cells, sergeants carrying shepherd's crooks in an attempt to symbolize the good shepherd or pastor. Of course, the functional role and aims of prisons in modern society differ from those of monasteries, so they've evolved in other directions.

(2) It's commonplace for prisoners to cover their basic expenses (tobacco, phone cards, coffee) by writing requests for charity to monasteries. Postal orders of ten, twenty, or even fifty euro arrive at prison on a daily basis.

Μονόζυγο (/mo'noziɣo/): pull-up bar. It's the most widely used workout equipment alongside the double push-up bars. Most of the time, they're tubes placed at various spots around the block, like the yard or the entertainment halls that serve as gyms. Throughout the day, there's nearly always someone hanging from these bars, doing his reps.

Μπακάλης (/ba'kalis/): grocer. Each prison has a contract with a supermarket that provides prisoners with what they need. Each prison has its own—irrational or not—prohibitions on certain products, but, in general terms, besides bottled water, cigarettes, and phone cards—which are provided by the canteen—prisoners can get hold of what the supermarket has to offer by placing an order once a week. The grocer and canteen usually deliver their orders on different days.

Μπατιρογαμιόλας (/batiroɣami'olas/): demeaning but cute way to call someone "poor and fucked up."[54]

Μπίλια (/'bilia/): literally, a marble ball. A body modification procedure commonly known as "pearling" that was most likely introduced to Greek prisons by Romanian prisoners. The ball is a penile implant technique that aims at redressing the consequences of long-term sexual abstinence.

What generally happens is the prisoner takes a nail clipper apart, uses the upper part as a chisel, places his penis on a solid surface—preferably a sink—and hammers the chisel with the

54. It's a compound noun made of two words, namely "μπατίρης" (/ba'tiris/) and "γαμιόλας" (/ɣami'olas/). The first stems from the Turkish word *batirmak* and means financially destroyed. The second means something like "fucker" in Greek.

help of a shaving gel bottle into the skin of his penis in order to create an incision. As soon as the incision is at place, he inserts the implant. It's usually a ball made from the end of a plastic toothbrush that's been chiseled and abraded with a marbling tool and a lighter until it's the approximate size and shape of a corn kernel. Once inserted, he covers his penis with bandages until the wound is healed.

As the story goes, it is supposed to improve sexual performance despite the pain it might inflict on the lover. Some prisoners have more than one ball or experiment with more aerodynamic shapes.

Μπίτζο (/'bijo/): friend in the Georgian language. It's a word very commonly used by Georgian prisoners and, thus, one used to address Georgians in general.

Μπλε κελιά (/ ble keli'a/): blue cells. They're disciplinary cells found in the psychiatric clinic of Korydallos prison. The walls are coated with blue foam boards in order to prevent prisoners from committing suicide by banging their heads against the walls. After the administration of a drug cocktail, of which Aloperidin is the most widely used and capable of causing temporary or permanent loss of consciousness, the prisoner is subject to a lengthy temperature fluctuation torture, ranging from very cold to very hot. This method of disciplinary torture is still in use.

Μπλιάτ (/bli'at/): whore in the Russian language. This word has the same meaning as "γαμώτο" [fuck] in Greek and is placed at the end of nearly all the utterances a Russian prisoner may articulate.

Μπράβος (/'bravos/): bouncer. The prisoner who is detained or serves a sentence for his involvement in underworld businesses like blackmailing, night club explosions, death pacts, protection racketing, etc. A bouncer usually belongs to a team that has its own internal hierarchy.

Νύχια (/'nihia/): nails. For prisoners it's common practice to cut their nails outside of their cells. Cuttings from fingernails and toenails are spread all over. It's not pleasant.

Όρνιο (/'ornio/): literally, vulture. A very widely used term, synonym of fool.

Ουίκου (/u'iku/): wolf in the Albanian language. It's a scream used by Albanian prisoners that signals a guard's unanticipated presence in a block, and thus prompts those engaged in prohibited actions to be mindful. In the past, Greek prisoners used to scream "guard" on similar occasions, but nowadays the distinction between service and prisoners for this race have started to fade.

Παλαιστικός (/palesti'kos/): wrestler-like, shredded. An adjective referring to anyone whose physique implies that he might be skilled at wrestling.

Παράνομος (/pa'ranomos/): outlaw. Those actively involved in the black market choose to define themselves as outlaws, avoiding the vilifying, journalistic or judicial terminology which brands them as "criminals." Of course, that's not the case for those who've committed an indictable offense on the spur of the moment, say for example, a crime of passion.

Πατρώνα (/pat'rona/): literally, a female patron. A Madam.[55] It's a pejorative characterization referring to guards, prison governors or thugs.

Πατσαβούρης (/patsa'vuris/): toe-rag. It's perhaps the most common disparaging option when it comes to name-calling.

Πειθαρχείο (/piθar'hio/), πειθαρχικό κελί (/piθarhi'ko ke'li/: see Κιούπι [the hole].

Πειθαρχικό (/piθarhi'ko/): disciplinary. It's a term that refers to indictable transgressions that result in some sort of disciplinary action. The punishment could be a temporary exclusion from labor days (up to two years), deprivation of leaves if committed while on leave (up to six months), a short-term confinement in the hole[56] or an adverse prison transfer, meaning the prisoner is transferred from prison to prison every few months for as long as the punishment lasts.[57] This process is remarkably tortuous since the prisoner can hardly acclimatize to an environment before getting transferred to yet another one.

---

55. As used in the context of brothels.
56. See "Κιούπι (/ki'upi/)": the hole [literally, a clay pot].
57. Known as "ghosting" in English.

Certain actions like prison break or attempted prison break, battering, attempted or committed homicide, and possession of narcotic substances can lead to penal consequences while others—like possession of a mobile phone or alcoholic beverages, verbal abuse against guards or insubordination—lead to "disciplinary" only.

Πετούγια (/pe'tuɣia/) or **Τρελοπετούγια** (/trelope'tuɣia/): literally, door handle. It's a term that has almost become extinct in Greek prisons. It's a way to address guards because they turn the door handle to lock you in the cell. In modern prisons door handles no longer exist as locking and unlocking is done electronically at the watch point.

Πράσο (/'praso/): literally, leek.[58] A buzzword for dope.

Πρόεδρος (/'proeδros/): president. It's the most common sarcastic title awarded to a prisoner who controls a block.

Προνόμιο (/pro'nomio/): privilege. Any respect for prisoners' rights as described in penal legislation is so rare that it is considered an extraordinary privilege.

Πτέρυγα (/'pteriɣa/): wing. Alternatively, block. Most prisons are divided into wings. The distribution of prisoners in different wings helps the prison service to manage the prisoners more efficiently since communication among them becomes rather difficult. So difficult, in fact, that each wing is like a different prison.

---

58. The vegetable; it's like a larger, milder spring onion.

This division follows a biopolitical scheme of control; it is implemented in accordance with race or level of trade-offs with the service. As a result, there are wings that are mainly Greek, mainly Albanian, mainly Russian and so on and so forth. Likewise, there are racially mixed wings which are basically regarded as protection wings because they host grasses, white-collar criminals, prisoners who are in danger if placed in other wings, as well as prisoners who deserve special treatment like politicians or notorious members of organized crime. Moreover, there are wings that host those who are under strong psychiatric drugs. This last segregation aims at nothing else but the prevention of drug dealing among prisoners. One of the methods to make prisoners cooperate with the service is to threaten to move them—or to actually move them—to a wing where the balance of power makes them feel vulnerable.

Πυγμαχάκι (/piɣma'haki/): literally, mini-wrestler. One who is referred to as such because of their competence in wrestling. Since they're directly linked with the black market, and by extension with prisons, martial arts like wrestling flourish in this environment. It's common to see athletes who excel in martial arts serve a prison sentence.

Ράδιο (/'raðio/): radio. A code word for mobile phones.

Ρεξ (/rex/): Rex. A derisive title awarded to guards who conduct extremely meticulous investigations. This meticulousness isn't triggered by any kind of professionalism or perversion. Rather, it's a manifestation of competitiveness among dealers[59] who wish to preserve their monopoly in the trade of prohibited possessions.

Ριχτάδικο (/rih'taδiko/): a way to refer to a financial fraud that is characterized by levels of complexity.

Ρόπαλο (/'ropalo/): cudgel. The guard who tortures and physically abuses prisoners in order to suppress them is called a cudgel. Nowadays, the violence used by prison service is relatively limited and is usually directed to prisoners with dark complexions, given that they are almost unable to make formal accusations or pursue any kind of retaliation.

Ρουφιάνος (/rufi'anos/): grass.
(1) A prisoner who provides the service with useful information about life in the wing. Most of the time, they're weak prisoners who are coerced into this behavior, not only due to their moral degradation but also due to what they get in exchange. For example, a place in a wing where they're not in danger, a labor post, some material provisions such as phone cards, tobacco, etc. The prison service makes sure the rest of the prisoners know who the grasses are, which is a fact that keeps them vulnerable and in need of protection. A grass is not the same as a "servicial."[60]

(2) It's a small piece of mirror that helps prisoners keep an eye on what's going on in the corridor. For example, they can check

59. ee "Βαπόρι (/va'pori/)": pusher; literally, steamboat.
60. See "Υπηρεσιακός (/ipiresia'kos/)": "servicial."

through their door viewers or door slots and see if there's an inspection, if a guard is approaching, etc.

Ρυζόγαλο (/ri'zoɣalo/): rice pudding. One of the most popular desserts in prison because it can be prepared with simple equipment and ingredients, especially milk, which is readily available as prison rations.

There are plenty of variations and recipes, like rice pudding with banana, coconut, cocoa, etc. Every prisoner takes great pride in his unique recipe and thinks it's the best. They're always eager to share their secrets and will do so even when not asked.

Σεβαστικός (/sevasti'kos/): mannerly. A jarring characterization addressed to a prisoner who treats not only the hierarchically superior but also the inferior with respect. Usually, he deserves respect too.

Σεντόνι (/se'doni/): bed sheet. Beyond its obvious use, a bed sheet can serve in many different ways: as partition, curtains or wallpaper, for instance. Moreover, since there are no ropes, bed sheets are torn in strips and braided together to serve as durable ropes.

Σκαστά (/skas'ta/): the nominal years of one's sentence, without counting the already served or to-be-served labor days in.

Σκίζεται (/'skizete/): literally, one's getting torn. He's on the toilet, he relieves himself, he defecates.

Σκουπόξυλο (/sku'poxilo/): broomstick. It's an absolutely basic component in many DIY creations. For weights it's a rest while for curtains and partitions a trail. Pieces of broomstick can become bases for shelves.

Σουβλί (/souv'li/): shank. A thin piece of iron with a pointed end and DIY handle used as a knife in conflicts, account settlings or death pacts.

Σούμποτεξ (/'subotex/): a frequently encountered and medically approved substitute for heroin.

Σοφία (/so'fia/): a nickname for life imprisonment.

Σπαθόλουρο (/spa'θoluro/): thug. It's one of the most common insults in Greek prisons. Because language and—by extension—slang are dynamic, σπαθόλουρο has evolved to mean pretentious masculinity; it is the bully who attacks only when he senses weakness but obeys the stronger bully unconditionally.

In the past, this word has been used to indicate that someone is a "servicial"[61]—the one in charge of the wing who is appointed by the service in exchange for various privileges.

Since servicials come across as bullies, σπαθόλουρο has come to mean the bully in this sense.

Στάση (/'stasi/): an act of protest, such as when prisoners refuse to return to their cells to get counted, normally just before the noon and bedtime counts. This protest can be symbolic, done

61. See "Υπηρεσιακός (/ipiresia'kos/)": "servicial."

in consultation with and tolerated by the service or take a more violent turn and result in an uprising.

Στάση φύλακα (/'stasi 'filaka/): the guard's watch point. In modern prisons, the watch point has taken the place of the iron gate of the wing.[62] It's a small space next to the entrance of the wing that is protected with bulletproof glass, a one-way mirror, and iron bars. There, the guard spends his shift invigilating the prisoners. Surveillance is achieved by means of patrols as well as a system of closed-circuit TV cameras. This type of control is based on the principles of panopticism, which means the prisoner does not know when he is being watched. Inside the cells there are no cameras.

The guard who spends his shift at the watch point is the front man for any communicative exchange a prisoner might wish to have with the prison service.

Σταυρός (/stav'ros/): cross. It used to be a method of disciplinary torture, which existed until the mid-nineties. The cross was found in the "hole."[63] It was adjusted at such height that would allow only a light touch of the toes on the ground. The practice could last for a few days and prisoners where unhanged only to eat and sleep. Usually, it was accompanied by beatings. Nowadays, the cross has been abolished and given its place to more civilized forms of disciplinary torture like the blue cells.

Στεγνή (steγ'ni/): literally, dry; figuratively, squeegee. Due to the abundance of water that prisoners use nowadays to clean both

62. See "Κιγκλίδα (/kig'lida/)": the entrance to an old prison block, which has nowadays given its place to the watch point.
63. See "Κιούπι (/ki'upi/)": the hole [literally, a clay pot].

blocks and cells, the squeegee is so essential when it comes to water removal that is considered a must-have prison accessory.

Συγχώνευση (/siɣ'honefsi/): merging. It's the prisoner's right to serve concurrent sentences for different offenses or involvement in different cases. If a prisoner serves a life imprisonment plus twenty-five years or two or more life imprisonments on top of the first, then he reaches the upper limit of confinement, which is twenty-five years of actual confinement. No matter what other offenses he might commit in the future, all sentences are merged.

The lifers' notorious expressions "I'll merge you down" or "you're just another merging" means I'll kill you without any adverse impact on my sentence. Likewise, "I'll put your name down on my merging list" is like saying "I'll put your name down on my blacklist." Of course, rarely do lifers ever make use of this privilege because there's always a leave to look forward to.

Another way to get your sentences merged is when you've served one sentence but you later got sentenced again for a different offense. If you've served many years for the first sentence, these years are counted, otherwise your stock of assigned confinement would be considered too big. Consequently, your second sentence is shorter. You're entitled to a generous discount just like a good customer.

Συμβούλιο της φυλακής (/sim'vulio tis fila'kis/): prison council.
The prison council consists of the prison's governor, the judge in charge, and a social worker. When there's no social

worker in prison, this position is rightfully covered by an accountant. The prison council is responsible for making decisions on all critical issues related to prisoners, such as their appointment to a labor post, leaves, suspensions, visits, etc. Typically the sergeant doesn't participate in the prison council but his informal opinion bears a far greater importance than any of the other three.

Συσίτιο (/si'sitio/): ration. The food provided by the prison service, which usually ranges from simply inferior to very poor quality. In most prisons, prisoners have the right and the means to prepare their food on their own although the vast majority cannot afford it. For breakfast, each prisoner is entitled to two glasses of milk or tea or to one piece of packaged butter and marmalade.

For lunch, there's normally legumes, chicken or pasta—except Sundays when the menu provides red meat. The legume lunch is a pleasant meal. For dinner, there's pie, pizza, orzo, spinach soup, omelet, etc. Dinner is usually inedible. Also, every prisoner is entitled to a loaf of bread daily. On Sundays, in addition to red meat, the menu includes a dessert which is sometimes edible. Most of the time, portions are provocatively inadequate.

Ταλαιπωρημένος (/talepori'menos/): shagged. Some prisoners are often called shagged; not out of mercy but some sort of recognition, rather. This term is normally addressed to those who have served many or harsh years in prison.

Ταλιμπάν (/tali'ban/): Taliban. That's what prisoners from North Africa, West and Central Asia are called altogether.

Syrians, Afghans, Pakistanis. It's the third-world proletariat, excluding the Blacks.

Ταξί (/ta'xi/): literally, taxi. The errand-boy. A term referring to a prisoner who makes deliveries in exchange for a reward, usually a small pouch of tobacco per week. The errand-boy queues at the canteen, the grocer's or the food ration on behalf of other prisoners. An errand-boy's service might expand to cooking, dish washing, cell cleaning or laundry in exchange for a 10-euro phone card per week. The difference between a taxi and a "prison wife"[64] is that the former is a step higher in the hierarchy since he's paid for his service.

Τατουάζ (/tatu'az/): tattoo. Although the art of deliberate decorative injection of indelible pigments into the skin has always been widespread in prisons, its techniques and aesthetics have hardly made any progress. It's true that there are, indeed, some tattoos that cannot be easily classified as either professional or prison-made. Taking into account the exiguous resources—a motor from a shaving machine, a spring from a Bic lighter and ink from a Bic pen—one can conclude that there are gifted tattoo artists in prison. Nevertheless, as a rule, the shapes and design of these tattoos denigrate, or even disgrace, the art of tattoos. The word MOTHER—in asymmetrical, lopsided capital letters—or a misspelled girlfriend's name are common examples of prison tattoos.

The worst tattoos, though, belong to Roma prisoners who go for whatever they find eye-catching in magazines, like

64. See "Λεγκένης (/le'genis/)": prison wife.

various sports shoes brands. Moreover, the tattoos are used as identifiers. The most common are the following:

A spider's web signifies that someone is an outlaw. Placing the spider closer to or further from the center signifies whether one is still active or not.

Three little dots usually marked between thumb and pointer finger, forming an imaginary triangle—quite known to people in the out—are said to represent the expression "cops, pigs, murderers"[65] or, according to another version, "see no evil, hear no evil, speak no evil."

Five dice-like dots mean the prisoner has spent some time in the disciplinary cell. The four surrounding dots represent the four walls while the one in the middle is a depiction of the prisoner himself.

A saint tattoo implies that one has served in "minors"[66] and it symbolizes the protector saint of all outlaws.

Russian prisoners, too, bear interesting tattoos, which signify their place within the hierarchy of their community and are usually the outcomes of an initiation process following a senior member's permission or prompting.

The following prison tattoos happen to exist: "Dad don't speed," "Jesus saves," "Oh poor father," "ONLY YOU, OH MOTHER, UNDERSTAND AND FORGIVE ME."

---

65. "Μπάτσοι, γουρούνια, δολοφόνοι" (/'batsi, γu'runia, dolo'foni/), the Greek equivalent for "All Cops Are Bastards" (ACAB).
66. See "Ανήλικα (/a'nilik/)."

Ταχυδρόμος (/tahi'ðromos/): postman. A nickname attributed to the guard who is in charge of posting, collecting, and delivering the prisoners' mail.

Τεμπέλης (/te'belis/): literally, lazy. It's a strap removed from a knapsack. Both ends are tied on the upper bed of a bunk bed, allowing the occupant who lies on the lower bed to rest his legs by placing them on the hammock-like curve it forms. Unfortunately, the beds on the top or the single ones cannot support this precious accessory. There's also a version for hand-resting but this is rather extreme as well as uncommon.

Τουμπεκής (/tube'kis/): literally, tobacco used in a Turkish water pipe. Figuratively, trustworthy. A prisoner who's proved that he's not a grass.

Τούφα (/'tufa/): literally, hairball. Figuratively, time spent in prison.[67]

Τριανταεξάρης (/ triadaek'saris/): thirty-sixer. Article 36 pertains to those who invoke the insanity defense at court. A thirty--sixer is a prisoner who made it to get subjected to this Article at court and, thus, be sentenced to a shorter sentence. Thirty-sixer also refers to an idiot or the deranged, in general.

Τρίπολη (/'tripoli/): Tripoli, a provincial Greek town. The prison in Tripoli is where rapists, pedophiles, etc. are placed. It's not an honorable destination.

---

67. It's equivalent to the English prison-lingo expression "I'm doing *bird* in prison."

Τρύπα (/'tripa/): hole. It's a widely used pejorative characterization, often pronounced as /'trupa/.

Τρυπάω (/tri'pao/): drill. A prisoner "drills" the prison when he manages to smuggle illegal commodities like drugs or mobile phones, often during a transfer from one prison to another, on his return from a leave or during a visit. Prisoners are very resourceful when it comes to such expedients. Tucking[68] is one of many drilling methods and is not particularly effective nowadays. The more modern methods ought to remain uncommented on. The ease with which each prison can be drilled, and the consequent methods that each prison service focuses on, engender a gradation system of "*drillability.*" An alternative method is that of "pushing."[69]

Τσάβο (/'tsavo/): child in Romani. It has evolved to mean any Roma individual.

Τσίπουρο (/'tsipuro/): brew. A prison-made alcoholic beverage made of fruit—mostly apples, oranges, and peaches since grapes are prohibited in prison for this very reason. The smashed fruit is placed in a container with some yeast, which is nothing more than moldy bread as proper yeast is prohibited. Then comes the boiling water followed by the sugar. The mixture should be kept as warm as possible with the use of either a blanket or another container with hot water.

Fermentation is completed almost within a week and the alcoholic mix looks like wine. Filtering is achieved with the use

---

68. See "Λουκαδώρος—Λουκάρω (/luka'ðoros—lu'karo/)": tucker—or, to tuck.
69. See "Βαπόρι (/va'pori/)": pusher; literally, steamboat.

of pillowcases. The dregs held in the pillowcase serve as yeast in future fermentations, which results in the yeast getting stronger and stronger. The—now filtered—alcoholic beverage is poured into a plastic bucket. At the upper part of this bucket there's a small plastic cup that is tied with the use of bed-sheet strips in such a way that it hovers inside the bucket and over the surface of the liquid. Finally, the bucket is sealed with airtight seal, which is an appropriately adjusted piece of plastic supermarket bag. The cup—also known as "thief"[70]—is dipped in the bucket while the surface of the plastic foil gets rinsed with tap water. This way, the container is warmed on the one side and cooled on the other, filling the adjusted cup with alcoholic drops. This is how distillation is accomplished.

This booze is of extremely low quality and, of course, particularly harmful to the consumer's health. However, it fulfills its principal aim, which is to cause an advanced state of inebriation. Distillation, possession, and consumption of alcohol are all transgressions that carry a disciplinary punishment. However, the prison service is, most of the time, quite lenient unless drunkenness results in prisoners getting completely out of line. It isn't rare for producers to sell their brew to make ends meet. Prices may fluctuate from two to four ten-euro phone cards.

Υλικό (/ili'ko/): material. It's the human geography or population mix in each wing. If a wing "has got material,"[71] this means the prisoners challenge and stand up against the prison service.

70. See "Κλέφτης ('kleftis/)": literally, thief.
71. "έχει υλικο," (/'ehi ili'ko/).

Υπάλληλος (/I'palilos/): staff. A term to refer to lowly ranked prison staff. Prison service consists of the prison staff—the sub-sergeants occupy the lowest ranks with the head sub-sergeant on the top—and the sergeant who manages all of them. Staff is the word prisoners choose to use when referring to both prison staff as well as sub-sergeants.

Υπηρεσία (ipire'sia/): service. All prison personnel, from the lowest ranks of prison staff to sergeants, and from the lowly ranked accountants to prison governors. Also, as an adjective, it modifies all prison provisions. The rations, for instance, are called "service food." The same applies for blankets, bed sheets, clothes and sanitary products given to poor prisoners. They all stand out for their poor quality.

Υπηρεσιακός (/ipiresia'kos/): "*servicial*." It's the prisoner who gets on well with the staff, especially the sergeant. Unlike a grass, he enjoys a place high in the hierarchy and ensures the wing functions properly. All this is in exchange for certain privileges, of course. He is not a grass.

Υπογράφω (/ipoγ'rafo/): sign.
(I) When a prisoner completes three-fifths of his nominal sentence, meaning when the sum of real served time plus labor days reaches three-fifths of the nominal sentence, then he's entitled to sentence suspension and conditional release. This is when he signs the terms of his suspension and looks forward to an attestation granted by the council in charge. The norm is for this attestation to be granted if the prisoner meets the

minimum formal requirements, meaning unless he's committed a disciplinarily punishable misdemeanor or there's a trial due for an offense that might potentially increase his sentence. The expressions *"I'm signing . . .* in two years, . . . next month . . . on Wednesday" mean "I will be soon reaching my suspension limit and am looking forward to my conditional release."

(2) I *"sign someone"* means "I've testified against someone," or conversely, "someone has testified against me." This often occurs among co-respondents. Prisoners *"sign one another"* very often in drug cases.

Φάρμακα (/'farmaka/): medicine. It refers to psychiatric medication, which is amply provided to prisoners to help them deal with the intense, prison-engendered stress.

Φορτωτική (/fortoti'ki/): loading. The brazenly long list of charges the police loads on someone in order to get the case closed. Sometimes it's done so sloppily that the very same person might be accused of two different offenses that took place at the same time but at different places.

Φούντος (/'fudos/): a drilling method.[72] Prohibited possessions like drugs, mobile phones, knives and rather rarely guns are hurled into the prison yard by someone in the out. More often than not, this service comes with charges. Tight surveillance and long distances between streets and prison yards—ensured by means of dead zones—have led this method into extinction.

72. See "Τρυπάω (/tri'pao/)": drill.

Φουσκωτός (/fusko'tos/): pumped up. It's a term to describe a burly and beefy prisoner who is usually—not necessarily— charged for night-underworld–related cases.

Φράσεις (/'frasis/): expressions. There are dozens of expressions that are common in prison but do not exist in the out. You will find the most common ones with their meaning below.

"Ο τσέτουλας, ο πέτουλας και ο χαρτοσακούλας" (/o 'tsetulas, o 'petulas ke o hartosa'kulas/). Alternatively, "ο τσέτουλας, ο πέτουλας, και ο γιος του σκοτωμένου" (/o 'tsetulas, o 'petulas ke o yi'os tu skoto'menu/).
>
> These expressions describe an assembly of individuals of low importance.
>
> It's similar to "η Σάρα και η Μάρα" (/i 'sara ke i 'mara).

"Έφαγε μαϊτάπι" (/'efaye mai'tapi).
>
> He's experienced something that . . . *is a bitch.*
>
> It's an archaic expression still used by older prisoners and resembles the more modern "έφαγε πακέτο" (/'efaye pa'keto/).

"Χρόνια καλά" (/'hronia ka'la/).
>
> An expression used when wishing someone *"quality years."* Given that *quantity* is bitterly mentioned at court, the equivalent common wish that pertains to quantity tends to be a taboo, thus the substitute focus locks on *quality.*

"Θα γαμηθείς" (/θa yami'θis/).
>
> The somewhat vague threat *"you'll get fucked"* normally prevails over the syntactical precision of the active voice (i.e., *"I'll* fuck you"). There are various versions like the

legendary *"you'll get fucked at the transfer cage."*[73] Transfer vans as well as court detention cells are places where prisoners from different prisons or wings meet, thus where stakeholders—otherwise unlikely to come across one another—settle their accounts. Other possible expressions are *"you'll get fucked . . . in a bewildering variety of ways,"* *"you'll get fucked . . . from head to toes,"* and *"you'll get fucked . . . with your elbows tied behind your back."*[74]

"Πουτάνα θάλασσα που σε γαμούν τα ψάρια" (/pu'tana 'θalasa pu se γa'moun ta 'psaria/).

Literally *"sea, oh you bitch, that all fish shall fuck you."* It's a surreal anathema, a diamond of folk culture.

"Όλοι οι πούστηδες τυχεροί είναι" (/'oli i 'pustiδes tihe'ri 'ine/).

"All faggots are lucky." It's the most common statement made by someone who loses in backgammon or any other game in which luck plays a vital role. The intent is to excuse one's loss and undermine the rival's skill.

"Γαμώ τα γαμήσια μου" (/γa'mo ta γa'misia mu/).

"Fuck my fuckoveries." Comments can be spared.

"Ο λόγος του και ο κώλος του το ίδιο πράγμα" (/ o 'loγos tu ke o 'kolos tu to 'iδio 'prama/).

"You can take either his word or his ass for it; it's all the same." This expression is credited to untrustworthy prisoners, staff, sergeants etc.

73. "Θα γαμηθείς στην κλούβα" (/θa γami'θis stin 'kluva/).
74. In the same order: "Θα γαμηθείς . . . πατόκορφα/ ποικιλοτρόπως/ πισθάγκωνα" (/θa γami'θis . . . Pikilot'ropos/ pa'tokorfa/ pis'θagona/).

"Μυρίζει μουνί" (/mi'rizi mu'ni/) and "κατουράει μπύρα" (/katu'rai 'bira/).

"He smells like pussy" and *"he pisses beer."*

Teasing expressions addressed to someone who is fresh in prison or has returned from a leave.

"Γαμώ τον εισαγγελέα που σ'έβαλε φυλακή" (/ɣa'mo ton isage'lea pu 'sevale fila'ki/).

"Fuck that judge who put you in prison."

It's an anathema cast on the culprit behind a prisoner's presence.

"Γαμώ το αδίκημά μου" (/ɣa'mo to a'ðiki 'mamu/).

"Fuck my offense."

"Γαμώ τη φυλακή που έχεις βγάλει" (/ɣa'mo ti fila'ki pu 'ehis 'vɣali/).

"Fuck the prison time you've served."

"Γαμώ τα ισόβιά σου" (ɣa'mo tai'so vi'asu/).

"Fuck your life imprisonment."

All these expressions are addressed to prisoners who are not to be treated with due respect despite the serious offenses they were charged with, the long sentences or life imprisonment they serve.

"Δεν τον βλέπω" (/ðen ton 'vlepo/).

"I don't see him."

It means I scorn someone, I don't take them into account.

"Στο πρωτόδικο δικάζουν για τους μπάτους, στο εφετείο για τον κατηγορούμενο" (/sto pro'toðiko ði'kazun ɣi'a tus 'batsus, sto efe'tio ɣi'a ton katiɣo'rumeno/).

"The Court of First Instance hosts a cops' show, the Court of Appeal hosts a trial." This expression crystallizes the prisoners' overall experience of Greek penal justice as well as the importance of the Court of Appeal.

"Τα μεροκάματα είναι το δεύτερο εφετείο" (/ta mero'kamata 'ine to 'deftero efe'tio/).
   "Labor days are a second Court of Appeal." An expression that shows how important labor days are to prisoners.

"Το καλύτερο παιδί. Σπίτι φυλακή, φυλακή σπίτι" (/to ka'litero pe'ði. spiti fila'ki, fila'ki 'spiti/).
   "He's his mom's pride. Home to prison, prison to home."
   An expression used to sarcastically describe one who is in and out of prison all the time.

"Γαμήσι, ξύλο και άπλωμα στον ήλιο." (/ɣa'misi, 'ksilo ki 'aploma ston 'ilio):
   "I'll whack you, leather you, and finish you off."
   It's either a threat or a description of lynching.

"Μη λερώνεις το στόμα σου" (/mi le'ronis to 'stoma su/) or "μη χαλάς το στόμα σου" (/mi ha'las to 'stoma su/).
   "Don't spoil your mouth" or *"Don't do a hatchet job on him."*
   It's a warning towards a prisoner who speaks badly of or slanders another prisoner.

"Γιατί γαμιούνται" (/ɣia'ti ɣami'ude/).
   "Coz they're fucked."
   It's the most common response to any complaint related to negligence, manipulation, vengefulness, etc. from the

prison service, judges or police authority.

A few exemplary exchanges:

"*Why did they put your leave on hold?—Coz they're fucked.*"

"*Why did they get you loaded with all these charges?—Coz they're fucked.*"

"*Why's the water off?—Coz they're fucked.*"

Often, the third exchange tends to be "από παλιά,"[75] which means "*same old story,*" and is accompanied by an empathetic nod.

"Στη φυλακή που βγάζω" (/sti fila'ki pu 'ngazo/).

"*I swear on the prison I serve.*" Perhaps the bleakest oath in the world.

"Του σηκώνεται από πίσω" (/tu si'konete a'po 'piso/).

"*He gets horny from behind.*" It's a common teasing expression that implies someone's homosexual orientation.

"Χαλιέμαι" (/hali'eme/).

Literally, *get spoiled.* Figuratively, swear at someone or don't even bother to swear at someone.

Alternatively, "Δεν θέλω να χαλαστώ" (/δen 'θelo na hala'sto/): "*I shrug the swearing off.*"

"Μη με πας ταξίδι" (/mi me pas tak'siδi/).

Literally, "*don't trip me round,*" meaning, "don't beat around the bush, don't coin excuses, speak the truth."

---

75. (/a'po pali'a/).

"Βγάζω τσέτουλο τούφα" (/'νγazo 'tsetulo 'tufa/).

"I shouldn't be doing this bird,"[76] meaning "I'm innocent" or "I got caught stupidly."

"Φούτου μούτου" (/'futu 'mutu/).

Supposedly said; to be phony; or generally, *a lie of poor quality.*

"Πολλή φυλακή" (/po'li fila'ki/).

"Loads of prison." An expression pronounced with a sigh when one realizes where he is, how long he's been there or how long he'll still be there for.

"Έχω πορεία" (/'eho po'ria/).

"I've got a long journey ahead," meaning I'm serving a long sentence and I've covered only a small part of it.

"Έπεσα" (/'epesa/).

Literally, fell.

"I fell in," meaning "I got into prison." For example:

"Πρωτόπεσα το '86" (/pro'topesa to oγ'δoda 'exi/): I *first fell* in in '86.

"Ξανάπεσα το '92" (/xa'napesa to ene'nida 'δio/): I *fell in again* in '92.

"Έχω πέσει τρεις φορές" (/'eho 'pesi tris fo'res/): *I've fallen in* three times.

"Περπατάει καλά" (/perpa'tai ka'la/) or "Δεν περπατάει καλά" (/δen perpa'tai ka'la/).

"He knows how to walk" or *"he doesn't walk properly."* Both

76. See "Τούφα (/'tufa/)": literally, hairball.

expressions comment on a prisoner's behavior as observed over a duration.

"*Φεύγω μετά λήξης*" (/'fevɣo 'meta 'lixis/) or "*Θα φύγω μετά λήξης*" (/θa 'fiɣo 'meta 'lixis/).

"*I'm/ I'll be released upon termination.*" When a prisoner can't be granted a conditional release—meaning a suspension upon completion of three-fifths of his sentence—due to disciplinary punishments, he knows he'll be released only after he's served as much time as his nominal sentence predicts. Also, when a prisoner's trial at the Court of Appeal is delayed, there's a chance that the final reduced sentence will have no effect on the actual time served because of the delay. Thus, he's released upon termination of his sentence. Another case is that of prisoners who happen to have served more time than the reduced sentence predicts. As a result, prisoners jokingly gauge the numbers of free years the Court owes them back.

"*Ο,τι γίνεται, μαθαίνεται*" (/'oti 'ɣinete ma'θenete/).

"*Whatever's up never goes unnoticed.*" A common response to the question "what's up?"[77] This implies prison is a small community where it's rare for information not to leak.

"*Τον έχω/ έχουν έτοιμο*" (/ton 'eho/ 'ehun 'etimo/).

"*I/They've set him all up.*" An expression that implies that someone is awaiting the slightest excuse to beat someone else up or stab him.

---

77. "*τι γίνεται;*" (/ti 'ɣinete/).

"Τον βαράγανε για να σταματήσει" (/ton va'raɣane ɣi'a na stama'tisi/).

"He had to get whacked up to shut the fuck up." This expression is used when describing a grass' attitude during interrogation. In the wonderland of outlaws, it's not rare for someone who is interrogated to start talking more than he's been asked to. This is either due to fear or because he's aiming to obtain a more lenient treatment at court. An outlaw who doesn't negotiate with the police is considered a rather phenomenal case, since negotiation with the police is an integral part not only of criminal justice but also of how the world of outlaws works, in general. As a result, if the police "needn't whack one up to make them stop grassing," then this is a satisfying outcome.

Φυλάκιση (/fi'lakisi/): See "κάθειρξη" (/'kaθirksi/): kathirksi.

Φυλή (/fi'li/): race. Nationality or race, if you like, is a fundamental—perhaps the ultimate—characteristic that the division of prisoners is based upon. On the one hand, this is a criterion prison service promotes/imposes when distributing prisoners in wings while, on the other, it's a means of turning races against one another in order to diminish their potential as a collective subject of authority. This tradition has been fully endorsed by prisoners; each race makes a self-contained community. The most populous race is the Albanian one while the most strictly and tightly organized is the Russian. The Russian community consists mostly of former USSR nationals like Pontics, Georgians, Kazakhs, Ukrainians, and Armenians. Each member of the Russian community has a distinct place within their internal hierarchy, which can be climbed up or, more rarely, down. Albanians, Russians, and Greeks are the three races that compete against one another over the control of prisons. Of course, there's great competition among the members of the same race as well. This is rather typical of the Greek community. The Kurdish and Arab communities are worth mentioning, population-wise. They're also the ones who negotiate the least with prison service but those who are the most loathed by the rest of the races. Roma, Blacks, and Pakistanis have the worst of fates inside prison, since they're the poorest, without good connections and thus, very low in the hierarchy's ranks. Other prisoners turn them into their errand-boys[78] or prison wives,[79] while prison service appoints them in the least favorable labor posts like cooking or cleaning garbage bins.

Ψυχιατρείο (/psihia'trio/): psychiatric asylum. The psychiatric unit of Korydallos prison. A place where torture and pharmaceutical experimentation take place. It's also a recreational destination for drug addicts, who cherish their transfer because they gain access to drugs.

Lately, it's also where people like businessmen, prison, and police staff—who for whatever reason find themselves in prison—find shelter when in need of protection. All the same, privileged prisoners can call on mental issues and get transferred from remote prisons to downtown Athens for some time—as much as their visits necessitate.

78. See "Ταξί (/ta'xi/)": literally, taxi.
79. See "Λεγκένης (/le'genis/)": prison wife.

The psychiatric unit of Korydallos prison crystallizes all the extreme class-based inequality among prisoners, given that some end up there to get tortured while others are there to enjoy recreation.

Appendix

A cell.

Squeegee, see "Στεγνή (steγ'ni/)," page 92.

A hammock-like strap, see "Τεμπέλης (/te'belis/)," page 96.

Even a small paper box may be used to save space inside the cells.

The sacred moment of defecation, the only moment a prisoner is alone.

The disciplinary wings of Korydallos prison.

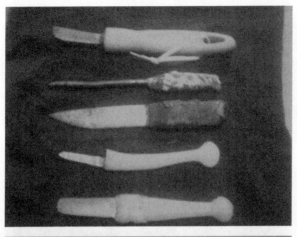

Knives and awls for all tastes.

Shank, see "Σουβλί (/souv'li/), page 90.

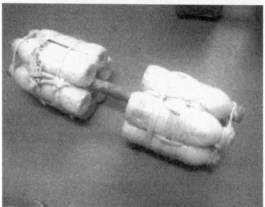

Improvised weights built from water bottles, strips of bed linen, and coarse salt.

Handiwork made with simple materials and a lot of patience.

An improvised frappe-making tool from straws, the base of a shaver, and a bottle cap.

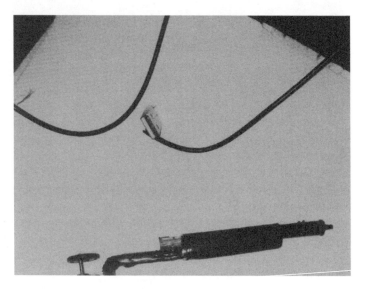

An improvised tattoo machine.

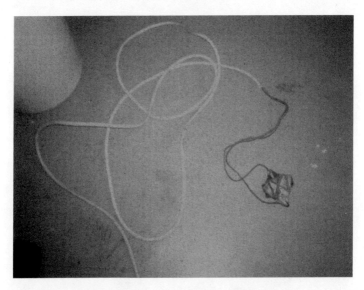

A prison-made electronic device used for distilling liquor, see
"Κλέφτης ('kleftis/)," page 74.

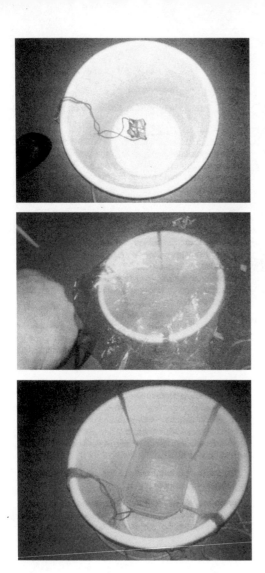

Different stages of making improvised *tsipouro*, a grape brandy.

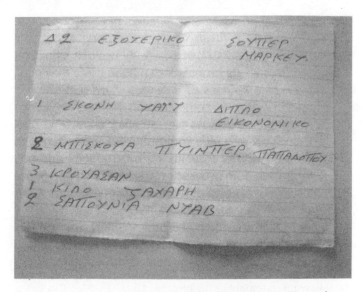

A typical grocery order: one Tide laundry detergent economy pack, two packages Papadopoulous Petit Beurre (Pti-ber) biscuits, three croissants, one kilogram sugar, two Dove soap bars.

About Tasos Theofilou

Tasos Theofilou is an anarchist-communist and political prisoner in Greece from 2012 to 2017. He is the author of eight books. Working across genres—in speculative fiction, noir, and the graphic novel—he illuminates the conditions of exploitation and social conflict in Greece. While in prison, Theofilou also authored a book on Attica as part of the international solidarity with the U.S. prisoners' strike on the forty-fifth anniversary of the uprising.

Theofilou addressed the Court of Appeal on April 28, 2017 with the following statement as his plea:

"My prosecution is part of a comprehensive effort by the Greek political personnel to introduce, implement, and enforce a law-and-order doctrine over the past two-and-a-half decades—an effort which has intensified from 2009 to 2015. This is a doctrine that entwines the Ministry of Public Order and the Ministry of Justice and is imported by the Greek government as a policy package from the United States.

I repeat once again, and conclude, that I did not commit the offenses for which I am accused. I did commit, however, the one offense that includes all others. I am an anarchist. In the class war, I chose the side of the excluded and the underprivileged, the prosecuted and the accursed, the poor, the weak, and the oppressed.

My imprisonment is, on the one hand, the only natural consequence of that choice, and on the other hand, one more field of struggle."

About Common Notions

Common Notions is a publishing house and programming platform that advances new formulations of liberation and living autonomy. Our books provide timely reflections, clear critiques, and inspiring strategies that amplify movements for social justice.

By any media necessary, we seek to nourish the imagination and generalize common notions about the creation of other worlds beyond state and capital. Our publications trace a constellation of critical and visionary meditations on the organization of freedom. Inspired by various traditions of autonomism and liberation—in the United States and internationally, historically and emerging from contemporary movements—our publications provide resources for a collective reading of struggles past, present, and to come.

Common Notions regularly collaborates with editorial houses, political collectives, militant authors, and visionary designers around the world. Our political and aesthetic interventions are dreamt and realized in collaboration with Antumbra Designs.

www.commonnotions.org
info@commonnotions.org

Monthly Sustainers

These are decisive times, ripe with challenges and possibility, heartache and beautiful inspiration. More than ever, we are in need of timely reflections, clear critiques, and inspiring strategies that can help movements for social justice grow and transform society. Help us amplify those necessary words, deeds, and dreams that our liberation movements and our worlds so need.

Movements are sustained by people like you, whose fugitive words, deeds, and dreams bend against the world of domination and exploitation.

For collective imagination, dedicated practices of love and study, and organized acts of freedom.
By any media necessary.
With your love and support.

Monthly sustainers start at $5, $10 and $25.

At $10 monthly, we will mail you a copy of every new book hot off the press in heartfelt appreciation of your love and support.

At $25, we will mail you a copy of every new book hot off the press alongside special edition posters and 50% discounts on previous publications at our web store.

Join us at commonnotions.org/sustain.

More From Common Notions

Abolishing Carceral Society
Abolition Collective

978-1-942173-08-3
$20.00
256 pages
20 Illustrations

Beyond border walls and prison cells—carceral society is every-where. *Abolishing Carceral Society* presents the bold and ruthless-ly critical voices of today's revolutionary abolitionist movements.

This collection of essays, poems, artworks, and interventions are brought together to create an inciteful articulation & col-laboration across communities, movements, and experiences embattled in liberatory struggle. In a time of mass incarcera-tion, immigration detention and deportation, rising forms of racialized, gendered, and sexualized violence, and deep ecolog-ical and economic crises, abolitionists everywhere seek to un-derstand and dismantle interlocking institutions of domination and create radical transformations.

More From Common Notions

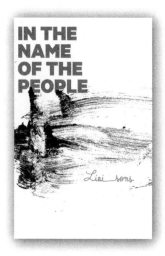

In the Name of the People
Liaisons

978-1-942173-07-6
$18.00
208 pages

The ghost of the People has returned to the world stage, claiming to be the only force capable of correcting or taking charge of the excesses of the time. This truly internationalist and collectivist publication boldly examines the forms of right and leftwing populism emergent in the fissures of the political world. Experimental in both form and analysis, *In the Name of the People* is the commune form of thought and text.

Colors of the Cage
Arun Ferreira

978-1-942173-13-7
$18.00
176 pages

A former political prisoner reveals the horrors he faced in prison and describes how countless others are facing similar situations all around India. This book is an eye-witness account of life in an Indian prison and the need for its abolition as part of a real democratic transformation of Indian society.

More From Common Notions

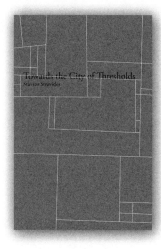

Towards the City of Thresholds
Stavros Stavrides

978-1-942173-09-0
$18.00
192 pages

Towards the City of Thresholds is a pioneering and ingenious study of new forms of socialization and uses of space—self-managed and communal—that passionately reveals cities as the sites of manifest social antagonism as well as spatialities of emancipation. Activist and architect Stavros Stavrides describes the powerful reinvention of politics and social relations stirring everywhere in our urban world and analyzes the theoretical underpinnings present in these metropolitan spaces and how they might be bridged to expand the commons.